THE BIRD.

THE BIRD

BY

JULES MICHELET.

WITH 210 ILLUSTRATIONS BY GIACOMELLI.

WILDWOOD HOUSE LONDON

First published in Great Britain by Thomas Nelson and Sons
in 1879

Re-issued in Great Britain by Wildwood House Limited 1981

Wildwood House Limited
Gloucester Mansions
Cambridge Circus
London WC2

Introduction copyright © by Philip Thody 1981

ISBN   0 7045 0444 8

Printed and bound in Great Britain by
The Camelot Press, Southampton

Translator's Preface.

THE reception accorded by the English press and public to the present translation has exceeded my most sanguine expectations, and calls for my most grateful acknowledgments. It is gratifying to find so large an audience prepared to welcome a non-scientific and purely sentimental illustration of the claims of the Animal World to man's consideration and sympathy. Zoological treatises by the ablest writers are to be found in every language, and the researches of comparative anatomists have led to very valuable and interesting results. But this is, perhaps, the first attempt that has been made by a man of genius to discover what we may call the *inner nature* of the animal, and reveal its feelings, passions, and higher impulses. We have the Bird brought before us in the following pages as a sentient being, with its duties to perform, its mission to fulfil. We are shown what it has to fear and what to hope ; what are the perils and what the consolations of its existence ; how it is inspired by love and jealousy ; how it possesses a faculty of combination and appreciation, of memory and reflection, which is something more than a cold mechanical instinct.

In fact, we are taught to regard it as closely allied to ourselves, as possessing endowments which we vainly long for, as occupying a position in the economy of Nature which closely concerns us ; and it is impossible to rise from a perusal of this Work without having acquired a new and living interest in the winged race.

" L'Oiseau," or " The Bird "—Michelet's first contribution to the sentimental illustration of Natural History—was published in 1856, and has passed through nine or ten editions in the French language. It has since been followed by " L'Insecte," " La Mer," and " La Montagne ; " the four composing a beautiful and perfect Whole, seldom surpassed in graphic vigour of style, tender feeling for Nature, and thoughtful suggestiveness.

In first submitting the following translation to the public, I stated that I was conscious of its many shortcomings. To do justice to Michelet in English was, in truth, no easy task ; yet if I had failed to convey a just idea of his beauties of expression, if I had suffered most of the undefinable *aroma* of his style to escape, I knew that I had done my best to render his meaning faithfully, without exaggeration or diminution. I sedulously endeavoured to preserve his more characteristic peculiarities, and even mannerisms : for in copying the masterpiece of a great artist, what we ask of the copyist is, that he will reproduce every effect of light and shade with the utmost faithfulness ; and in the translation of a noble work from one language to another, the public have a right to insist upon an equally exact adherence to the original. They want to see as much of the author as they can, and as little as may be of the translator.

This new edition has been carefully revised, but without any departure from the rules on which the translation was originally made. An Index has been added, and an Analysis of Subjects, which, it is believed, the reader will find of service.

Of the Illustrations, whose grace and finish have been universally acknowledged, and their fidelity to Nature liberally praised, it is enough to say that they are the work of Giacomelli, already known to the English public as the collaborateur of Doré in his celebrated edition of the Bible.

W. H. DAVENPORT ADAMS.

Introduction to the Wildwood House Edition

Lord Melbourne once said that he wished he could be as certain about anything as Lord Macaulay was about everything. The modern reader who opens Jules Michelet's *The Bird*, first published in 1856, when the historian was 58, is often tempted to say that he wished he could be as optimistic about anything as Michelet was about everything.

For Michelet soon recovers from the Tennysonian vision of 'Nature red in tooth and claw' inspired in him by the examination of a viper's head or the weapons of the bird of prey, what he calls those 'terrible beaks which kill with a blow . . . those talons, those sharpened claws, those instruments of torture which fix the shuddering prey, protract the last keen pangs and the agony of suffering.' For progress is on its way, and as 'nature gravitates towards a less violent order', the eagle is 'seldom met with, even among the Alps', while the falcon 'the noblest of the raptores, has nowadays nearly disappeared'. In contrast, as Michelet is pleased to note, the useful vulture is still around. By cleaning up the dead bodies which might otherwise spread infection, this bird is the 'servant of Life', and the Egyptians recognize the providential nature of its existence by the reverence they extend to 'these admirable agents of that beneficial chemistry which preserves and balances life here below'. Although beasts may be only machines — a surprising concession that the animal-loving Michelet makes to the traditional Cartesianism of his native land — their instinct invariably leads them to act in a way which is beneficial not only to themselves and to other creatures, but to human beings as well.

Neither is the optimism with which Michelet regards nature limited to the bird, the animal whose marvellous gift of flight makes man long to imitate its soaring power. Michelet's concept of Nature is unashamedly anthropomorphic and teleological. Birds, he declares in his study of the insect, 'kill by preference the most injurious insects', and when the bosom of the earth 'heaved with the glow of her first youth', both birds and insects combined to make it a more suitable dwelling place for man. For while, from above, the birds carried off the 'great-bellied reptiles, unwieldy frogs, green caymans and serpents swollen with filth and venom' which then inhabited our globe, the insects waged a similar war on this 'abominable fecundity' from below. And had not these 'myriads of nibblers . . . lightened the accumulation, cleansed the frightful lairs and thrown open to the arrows of the sun the filth under which the earth was panting', chaos would have continued to reign. Neither has Nature ceased to be equally providential now that order has finally arrived. Without the great Guiana ants, 'no effectual means would exist of thoroughly cleansing the homes of man from all the obscure broods which infest the shadows', and in the West Indies, the great spiders 'labour very industriously to secure the cleanliness of human habitations'. Even in our more temperate clime, 'fifty species of insects, in fellowship with ourselves', labour to destroy the 'useless, pungent, and in every sense disagreeable nettle', and Michelet's trust in providence and progress extends even beyond the impact which Nature has on the human realm. Black widow spiders, he is convinced, would not devour their mates if they lived in 'climates where ease and abundance did not deprave their natural disposition'.

It is tempting at first sight to attribute this unquenchable optimism less to Michelet himself than to his second wife, Athénais Mialaret. He had married her in 1848, when he was fifty and she twenty, and it has been suggested that it was she who wrote the books on natural history — *The Bird*, 1856; *The Insect*, 1857 — to which Michelet added his name and a few touches of style. Yet although this may be true on the level of anecdote, there is little in Michelet's much more important work as one of the most famous of French nineteenth-century historians to suggest that he had a more mitigated belief in the workings of Providence. Early in his career, in 1827, he produced a translation of the eighteenth-century Neapolitan historian Giambathista Vico's *Scienza prima nuova*, first published in 1725. Vico's concept of history as the passage from the Age of Gods to the Age of Heroes and from the Age of Heroes to the Age of Men made a lasting impact on this child of the Enlightenment who had absorbed a comparable gospel of progress from his father, a small printer who had gone bankrupt and been imprisoned for debt in 1808 when the more rigorous financial policies of Napoleon meant that there were fewer and fewer revolutionary *assignats* to print. Michelet saw history not only as the 'total resurrection of the past' but as a gradual liberation of man from the weight of fatality. The revolution of 1789 marked, for him, the beginning of the modern age, the moment when the reign of justice, incarnated in the people, replaced the reign of grace, represented by kings and priests.

'I do not believe', he wrote in his *Histoire de la Révolution Française*, published in seven volumes between 1847 and 1853, 'that the heart of man was ever at any time more open or more generous, that distinctions between classes, fortunes and parties were ever more forgotten, than in the early years of the Revolution. In villages especially, rich or poor, noblemen or commoners, ceased to be separated from one another; food was shared by all, tables were open to all.

Man, who in our old churches cannot recognize himself face to face, now becomes aware of his own being. He sees nature, he recovers possession of it, finds it to be sacred, and gives it a name: the fatherland.'

Whatever may subsequently have gone wrong in the Revolution, Michelet is convinced that it cannot be the fault of the people. Even the revolutionary wars do not dim its glory, however disastrous were the effects of the coming to power of Napoleon Bonaparte in 1799. He summarizes the military events of the Revolution and Empire by writing that, 'From 1793 to 1815, France gave the lives, for Belgium and for the world, of ten million of her children.' Neither were the Terror or the prison massacres of 1792 really the fault of 'this most intelligent of all populations, that of Paris.' If — as was rarely the case — these disasters were not actually caused by the priests, responsibility could still be laid firmly at the door of nefarious priestly intrigues. The 'Jacobin inquisition' in no way expressed the nature of the people, and it was the spirit of the Middle Ages which came alive again when the Convention of 1792 took on the aspect of the Councils of the Church which had defined and persecuted heresy in the past. All indeed would have been well, in Michelet's view, had not the essential goodness of the people been exploited by priests, and the Revolution itself 'enveloped in an immense Royalist conspiracy'. Just as Nature struggles ever forward towards less cruelty and in the direction of more light, so history itself finds its true expression in an 'eternal July' of which the French people is the perpetual hero.

Michelet's reference is to the 'three glorious days' in July 1830 when the people of Paris rose again in rebellion and finally drove out the last of the Bourbons. Michelet felt that France was then at last back on the right track, after the tyranny of the Napoleonic adventure, the Restoration of 1815, and the attempt by Charles X to go back to the *ancien régime*. In 1831, in the more liberal atmosphere of the July Monarchy, he published his *Histoire Romaine*, and in 1833 the first two volumes of his *Histoire de France*. In these and subsequent volumes, it was the People who became the real hero of events, never doubting the right of Joan of Arc to see herself as the true representative of its deepest aspirations, expressing itself in the upsurges of collective enthusiasm which led to the Crusades, the building of the great Gothic cathedrals, the spread of the Reformation — 'Luther', wrote Michelet 'was one of Us' — and the taking of the Bastille. From 1838 until 1851, Michelet preached a comparable gospel of anti-clercal, anti-Royalist, progressive optimism, with Kings, Jesuits and English gold as the enemies of France and the People as the incarnation of the providential will to freedom which gives meaning to history.

Then, almost as an answer to his prayer and a confirmation of his vision, came the revolution of February 1848 which drove out Louis Philippe and restored the Republic as the true government of France. Michelet made up a vast plan of universal, democratic education, and considered writing a religious epic of progressive optimism, *La Bible du Peuple*. When the hopes of a genuine democracy in France rapidly disappeared with the plebiscite which confirmed Louis Napoleon in the military dictatorship which he had established by the *coup d'état* of December 2nd, 1851, Michelet was discouraged but not downcast. It was, he wrote, the fault of the intellectuals who, like himself, had not done enough to educate the people, and who were thus punished by the way it had approved of the attempt by Napoleon's nephew to restore the grandeur of Imperial France.

Unlike Victor Hugo, with whom he shared a pact of mutual admiration, Michelet did not go into exile in protest against the destruction of French democracy. He refused to take the oath of allegiance to Napoleon III, was consequently dismissed from his Chair at the College de France, and left his native Paris. With Athénais Mialaret, he lived in Nantes, and it was while in the country that he published his books on natural history: *The Bird*, in 1856; *The Insect*, in 1857; *The Sea*, in 1861; and *The Mountain*, in 1868. Yet while he undoubtedly found in nature some consolation for the disappointment of his political hopes, he by no means changed his mind on the inevitability of human progress. The last two volumes of his *Histoire de la Révolution Française* were completed in 1852 and 1853, and in 1868 he published *La Bible de l'Humanité*, a history of religion of which Prometheus was the hero, and in which the cause of 'rightful emancipation' is depicted as being inevitably bound to triumph as a result of his spirit of eternal revolt. Only at the very end of his life, when the militarized Prussia of Bismarck defeated France in 1870 and united Germany behind her leadership, did Michelet's optimism begin to fade. The first three volumes of his *Histoire du XIXe siècle*, written in the last years of his life, take the story only as far as Waterloo, but already present a century increasingly 'dominated by fatality'. He died at Hyères, in the South of France, on February 6th, 1874.

A number of intellectual obstacles thus stand between the modern English reader and an enthusiastic admiration for Michelet as a historian and a thinker. Admittedly, he was on the side of the angels, perhaps more so than any other historian. He is now widely read again in France, with his books made available in cheap, paperback editions, and one of his modern commentators, Pierre Viallaneix, admiring him for having foreshadowed the dream of the revolutionary students of 1968 who wanted to give 'all power to the imagination'. In the immediate context of French intellectual history, he might even be regarded as having won. When, in 1881, the French established the system of compulsory state education which still provides the framework for what happens today, they deliberately excluded all religious instruction from state-subsidized schools. In 1905, France also became a secular Republic, and Michelet must have slept happier in his grave in the knowledge that priests and Jesuits were thus officially excluded both from public affairs and from the chance of influencing the young people of France. But it is more difficult to see how his vision of history as the continued liberation of humanity could have come to terms with Hitler, Stalin and Mao Tse Tung, to say nothing of Mr. Brezhnev.

Anyone who has digested the implications of the horror which Charles Darwin felt at the 'clumsy, wasteful, blundering, low and horribly cruel works of nature' will also read *The Bird* and *The Insect* with more appreciation for their poetic qualities and ecological enthusiasm than for Michelet's statement that he 'believes in but one miracle, the constant miracle of the Providence of Nature.' When *The Bird* was first published, Michelet's fellow historian, Hippolyte Taine, wrote that 'the author has not abandoned his career, he has widened it. Up to now, he has pleaded on behalf of humble folk, for simple folk, for children, for the people. He now pleads on behalf of beasts and birds', and it is certainly pleasant both to read this homage by one of the harder-headed French historians and to discover for ourselves in Michelet an author who can see so much goodness everywhere. But it would be very difficult, were it not for one theme, to see Michelet as anything other than an author in whom all the most dated attitudes of the nineteenth century reach their fullest development, and whose republication in English is an act of homage to one of the most famous and influential figures of the last century rather than a contribution to the intellectual life of the nineteen-eighties.

That theme is one that I have already mentioned: ecology. 'If a single species of ant should disappear', Michelet writes in *The Insect*, 'their loss would be serious, and cause a serious gap in the universal economy', and in *The Bird* he extends a similar concern to the whale. 'Those lords of the ocean', he writes, 'those mild and sagacious creatures which Nature has endowed with blood and milk — I speak of the cetacea — to how small a number are they reduced.' The language in which he speaks may be highflown and unfamiliar, and the limitations of his vision — as when he applauds the disappearance of eagles and falcons — a shade surprising to the more tolerant and comprehensive attitude which informs modern ecology. But there is no doubt that when Michelet talks of 'the natural union, the pre-existent alliance which prevails between us and these creatures of instinct, which we call *inferior*', he is writing with the same awareness which the late twentieth-century ecologist has of the symbiotic relationship between man and the natural world. When he deplores what he calls 'man's lack of sagacity in his campaigns against the birds', when he points out to the hunters that 'a terrible sentence of the Creator weighs upon the tribes of sportsmen — *they can create nothing*', he is also showing us how long standing is man's abuse of Nature and how relentlessly it is destroying that 'useful equilibrium of life and death' to which we all owe our existence.

The intellectual background to the vision of the human and natural world which gives certain passages in Michelet's work such an attractively modern a tone is not, as I have suggested, one that modern readers can accept very easily. Just as we find it hard to entertain a view of history which has such obvious villains and so comfortably guaranteed a happy ending, so our concept of nature is both cooler and less exciting than the one provided by Michelet's determination to see the hand of providence everywhere. The best we can do, if we resist the black romanticism of our own day which depicts nature as actually hostile to man, is accept that it is neutral. But it is a neutrality which we infringe at our peril, and which Michelet urges us to respect as much from motives of self-interest as out of a belief in the underlying purposes of which he was so certain.

Philip Thody.
1981

Contents.

———o———

CONTENTS.

List of Illustrations.

———o———

DRAWN BY H. GIACOMELLI:

ENGRAVED BY ETTLING, LAPLANTE, LALY, MADAME ROUGET, THENARD, GAUCHARD,
PANNEMAKER, BERVEILLER, MEUNIER, HILDEBRAND, MORICE,
HUREL, HURCHOLLE, ROUGET, AND SARGENT.

LIST OF ILLUSTRATIONS.

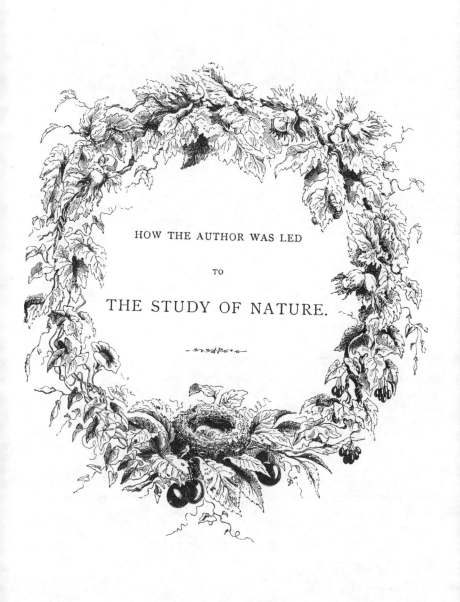

HOW THE AUTHOR WAS LED

TO

THE STUDY OF NATURE.

THE BIRD.

HOW THE AUTHOR WAS LED TO THE STUDY OF NATURE.

O my faithful friend, the Public, who has listened to me for so long a period without disfavour, I owe a confession of the peculiar circumstances which, while not leading me altogether astray from history, have induced me to devote myself to the natural sciences.

The book which I now publish may be described as the offspring of the domestic circle and the home fireside. It is from our hours of rest, our afternoon conversations, our winter readings, our summer gossips, that this book, if it be a book, has been gradually evolved.

Two studious persons, naturally reunited after a day's toil, put together their gleanings, and refreshed their hearts by this closing evening feast.

Am I saying that we have had no other assistance? To make

such a statement would be unjust, ungrateful. The domesticated swallows which lodged under our roof mingled in our conversation. The homely robin, fluttering around me, interjected his tender notes, and sometimes the nightingale suspended it by her solemn music.

The burden of the time, life, labour, the violent fluctuations of our era, the dispersion of a world of intelligence in which we lived, and to which nothing has succeeded, weighed heavily upon me. The arduous toils of history found occasional relaxation in friendly instruction. These pauses, however, are only periods of silence. Where shall we seek repose or moral invigoration, if not of nature ?

The mighty eighteenth century, which included a thousand years of struggle, rested at its setting on the amiable and consoling, though scientifically feeble book of Bernardin de St. Pierre.* It ended with that pathetic speech of Ramond's : " So many irreparable losses lamented in the bosom of nature !"

We, whatever we had lost, asked of solitude something more than tears, something more than the dittany † which softens wounded hearts. We sought in it a panacea for continual progress, a draught from inexhaustible fountains, a new strength, and—wings.

This work, whatever its character, possesses at least the distinction of having entered upon life under the usual conditions of existence. It results from the intimate communion of two souls; and is in all

* The book referred to was the " Études de la Nature."—*Translator*.
† Dittany was formerly much used as a cordial and sedative.—*Translator*.

things itself uniform and harmonious because the offspring of two different principles.

Of the two souls to which it owes its existence, one was the more powerfully attracted to natural studies by the fact that, in a certain sense, it had been born among them, and had ever preserved their fragrance and sweet savour. The other was so much the more strongly impelled towards them because it had always been separated by circumstances, and detained in the rugged ways of human history.

History never releases its slave. He who has once drunk of its sharp strong wine will drink thereof till his death. I could not wrench myself from it even in days of suffering. When the sorrows of the past blended with those of the present, and when on the ruins of our fortunes I inscribed "ninety-three," my health might fail, but not my soul, my will. All day I applied myself to this last duty, and pressed forward among the thorns. In the evening I listened—at first not without effort—to the peaceful narrative of some naturalist or traveller. I listened and I admired, unable as yet to console myself, or to escape from my thoughts, but, at all events, keeping them under control, and preventing any anxieties and any mental storms from disturbing this innocent tranquillity.

Not that I was insensible to the sublime legends of those heroic men whose labours and enterprise have so largely benefited humanity. The great national patriots whose history I was relating were the nearest of kindred to these cosmopolitan patriots, these citizens of the world.

For myself, I had long hailed, with all my heart, the great French
Revolution which had occurred in the Natural Sciences—the era of
Lamarck and of Geoffroy Saint-Hilaire,* so fertile in method, the
mighty restorers of all science.   With what happiness I traced their
features in their legitimate sons—those ingenious children who have
inherited their intellect !

At their head let me name the amiable and original author of the
" Monde des Oiseaux," † whom the world has long recognized as one
of the most solid, if not also the most amusing, of naturalists.   I
shall refer to him more than once ; but I hasten, on the threshold of
my book, to pay this preliminary homage to a truly great observer,
who, in all that concerns his own observations, is as weighty, as
special, as Wilson or Audubon.

    * Jean Baptiste de Monet, Chevalier de Lamarck, was born August 1, 1744 ; died
December 20, 1829.   His chief work is his " History of Invertebrate Animals."—Etienne
Geoffroy Saint-Hilaire was born in 1772, and died in 1844.   He expounds his theory of
natural history in the " Philosophie Anatomique," 2 vols., 1818–20.—*Translator*.

    † Alphonse Toussenel, an illustrious French *littérateur*, born in 1803.   The first edition
of his " Le Monde des Oiseaux, Ornithologie Passionelle," was published in 1852.—
Translator.

He has wronged himself by saying that, in his noble work, "he has only sought a pretext for a discourse on man." On the contrary, numerous pages demonstrate that, apart from all analogy, he has loved and studied the Bird for its own sake. And it is for this reason that he has surrounded it with so many legends, with such vivid and profound personifications. Each bird which Toussenel treats of is now, and will for ever remain, a person.

Nevertheless, the book now before the reader starts from a point of view which differs in all things from that of our illustrious master.

A point of view by no means contrary, yet symmetrically opposed, to his.

For I, as much as possible, seeking only the bird *in* the bird, avoid the human analogy. With the exception of two chapters, I have written as if only the bird existed, as if man had never been.

Man! we have already met with him sufficiently often in other places. Here, on the contrary, we have sought an *alibi* from the human world, from the profound solitude and desolation of ancient days.

Man could not have lived without the bird, which alone could save him from the insect and the reptile; but the bird had lived without man.

Man or no man, the eagle had reigned on his Alpine throne. The swallow would not the less have performed her yearly migration. The frigate bird,* unseen by human eyes, had still hovered over the

* The frigate bird, or man-of-war bird (*Trachypetes aquila*).—*Translator.*

lonely ocean-waters. Without waiting for human listeners, and with all the greater security, the nightingale had still chanted in the forest his sublime hymn. And for whom? For her whom he loves, for his offspring, for the woodlands, and, finally, for himself, his most fastidious auditor.

Another difference between this book and that of Toussenel's is, that, harmonious as he is, and a disciple of the gentle Fourier, he is not the less a *sportsman*. In every page the military calling of the Lorraine is clearly visible.

My book, on the contrary, is a book of peace, written specifically in hatred of sport.

Hunt the eagle and the lion, if you will ; but do not hunt the weak.

The devout faith which we cherish at heart, and which we teach in these pages, is, that man will peaceably subdue the whole earth, when he shall gradually perceive that every adopted animal, accustomed to a domesticated life, or at least to that degree of friendship or neighbourliness of which its nature is capable, will be a hundred times more useful to him than if he had simply cut its throat.

Man will not be truly man—we return to this topic at the close of our volume—until he shall labour seriously to accomplish the mission which the earth expects of him :

The pacification and harmonious communion of all living nature.

" A woman's dreams !" you exclaim. What matters that ?

Since a woman's heart breathes in this book, I see no reason to reject the reproach. We accept it as an eulogy. Patience and gentleness, tenderness and pity, and maternal warmth—these are the things which beget, preserve, develop a living creation.

May this, in due time, become not a book, but a reality ! Then, haply, it shall prove suggestive, and others derive from it their inspiration.

The reader, *au reste*, will better understand the character of the work, if he will take the trouble to read the few pages which follow, and which I transcribe word for word.

[The succeeding section, as the reader will perceive, is written by Madame Michelet.]

"I was born in the country, where I have passed two-thirds of my life-time. I feel myself constantly recalled to it, both by the charm of early habits, by natural sensibilities, and also, undoubtedly, by the dear memories of my father, who bred me among its shades, and was the object of my life's worship.

"Owing to my mother's illness, I was nursed for a considerable period by some honest peasants, who loved me as their own child. I was, in truth, their daughter; and my brothers, struck by my rustic ways, called me *the Shepherdess*.

"My father resided at no great distance from the town, in a very pleasant mansion, which he had purchased, built, and surrounded by plantations, in the hope that the charms of the spot might console his young wife for the sublime American nature she had recently quitted. The house, well exposed on the east and south, saw the morning sun rise on a vine-clad slope, and turn, before its meridian heats, towards the

remote summits of the Pyrenees, which were visible
in clear weather. The young elm-trees of our own
France, mingled with American acacias, rose-laurels, and
young cypresses, interrupted its full flood of light, and
transmitted to us a softened radiance.

"On our right, a thicket of oaks, inclosed with a
dense hedge, sheltered us from the north, and from the
keen wind of the Cantal. Far away, on the left, swept
the green meadows and the corn-fields. Through the
broom, and in the shade of some tall trees, flowed a
brooklet—a thin thread of limpid water, defined against
the evening horizon by a small belt of haze which ran
along its border.

"The climate is intermediate. In the valley, which
is that of the Tarn, and which shares the mildness of
the Garonne and the severity of Auvergne, we find
none of those southern products common everywhere
around Bordeaux. But the mulberry, and the melting
perfumed peach, the juicy grape, the sugared fig, and
the melon, growing in the open air, testify that we are
in the south. Fruits superabounded with us ; one
portion of the estate was an immense vineyard.

"Memory vividly recalls to me all the charms of
this locality, and its varied character. It was never
otherwise than grave and melancholy in itself, and it
impressed these feelings on all about it. My father,
though lively and agreeable, was a man already aged,
and of uncertain health. My mother, young, beautiful,
austere, had the queenly bearing of the North American,
with a prudence and an active economy very rare in
Creoles. The estate which we occupied formerly belonged

to a Protestant family, and after passing through
many hands before it fell into ours, still retained the
graves of its ancient owners—simple hillocks of turf,
where the proscribed had enshrined their dead under a
thick grove of oaks. I need hardly say, that these trees
and these tombs, consecrated by their very oblivion,
were religiously respected by my father. Each grave
was marked out by rose-bushes, which his own hands
had planted. These sweet odours, these bright blossoms,
concealed the gloom of death, while suffering, nevertheless, something of its melancholy to remain. Thither,
then, we were drawn, and as it were in spite of ourselves, at evening time. Overcome by emotion, we
often mourned over the departed ; and, at each falling
star, exclaimed, ' It is a soul which passes !' *

    " In this living country-side, among alternate joys
and pains, I lived for ten years—from four to fourteen.
I had no comrades. My sister, five years older than
myself, was the companion of my mother when I was
still but a little girl. My brothers, numerous enough
to play among themselves without my help, often left
me all alone in the hours of recreation. If they ran off
to the fields, I could only follow them with my eyes.
I passed, then, many solitary hours in wandering near
the house, and in the long garden alleys. There I
acquired, in spite of a natural vivacity, habits of con-

    * Alluding to a popular superstition, which Béranger has made the
subject of a fine lyric :—

        " What means the fall of yonder star,
            Which falls, falls, and fades away ?......
        My son, whene'er a mortal dies,
            Earthward his star drops instantly."—*Translator.*

templation. At the bottom of my dreams I began to feel the Infinite : I had glimpses of God, of the paternal divinity of nature, which regards with equal tenderness the blade of grass and the star. In this I found the chief source of consolation; nay, more, let me say, of happiness.

"Our abode would have offered to an observant mind a very agreeable field of study. All creatures under its benevolent protection seemed to find an asylum. We had a fine fish-pond near the house, but no dove-cot; for my parents could not endure the idea of dooming creatures to slavery whose life is all movement and freedom. Dogs, cats, rabbits, guinea-pigs, lived together in concord. The tame chickens, the pigeons, followed my mother everywhere, and fed from her hand. The sparrows built their nests among us ; the swallows even brooded under our barns; they flew into our very chambers, and returned with each succeeding spring to the shelter of our roof.

"How often, too, have I found, in the goldfinches' nests torn from our cypress-trees by rude autumnal winds, fragments of my summer-robes buried in the sand ! Beloved birds, which I then sheltered all unwittingly in a fold of my vestment, ye have to-day a surer shelter in my heart, but ye know it not !

"Our nightingales, less domesticated, wove their nests in the lonely hedge-rows ; but, confident of a generous welcome, they came to our threshold a hundred times a-day, and besought from my mother, for themselves and their family, the silk-worms which had perished.

"In the depths of the wood the woodpecker laboured obstinately at the venerable trunks; one might hear him at his task when all other sounds had ceased. We listened in trembling silence to the mysterious blows of that indefatigable workman mingling with the owl's slow and lamentable voice.

"It was my highest ambition to have a bird all to myself—a turtle-dove. Those of my mother's—so familiar, so plaintive, so tenderly resigned at breeding-time—attracted me strongly towards them. If a young girl feels like a mother for the doll which she dresses, how much more so for a living creature which responds to her caresses! I would have given everything for this treasure. But it was not to be so; and the dove was not my first love.

"The first was a flower, whose name I do not know.

"I had a small garden, situated under an enormous fig-tree, whose humid shades rendered useless all my cultivation. Feeling very sad and sorely discouraged, I descried one morning, on a pale-green stem, a beautiful little golden blossom. Very little, trembling at the lightest breath, its feeble stalk issued from a small basin excavated by the rains. Seeing it there, and always trembling, I supposed it was cold, and provided it with a canopy of leaves. How shall I express the transports which this discovery awakened? I alone knew of its existence; I alone possessed it. All day we could do nothing but gaze at each other. In the evening I glided to its side, my heart full of emotion. We spoke little, for fear of betraying ourselves. But ah! what

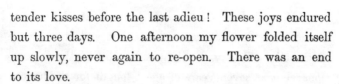

tender kisses before the last adieu! These joys endured
but three days. One afternoon my flower folded itself
up slowly, never again to re-open. There was an end
to its love.

"I kept to myself my keen regret, as I had kept
my happiness. No other flower could have consoled
me; a life more full of life was needed to restore the
freedom of my soul.

"Every year my good nurse came to see me,
invariably bringing some little present. On one occasion, with a mysterious air, she said to me, 'Put thy
hand in my basket.' I did so, expecting to find some
fruit, but felt a silken fur, and something trembling.
Ah! it is a rabbit! Seizing it, I ran in all directions
to announce the news. I hugged the poor animal with
a convulsive joy, which nearly proved fatal to it. My
head was troubled with giddiness. I could not eat.
My sleep was disturbed by painful dreams. I saw my
rabbit dying; I was unable to move a single step to
succour it. Oh! how beautiful it was, my rabbit, with
its pink nose, and its fur as polished as a mirror! Its
large pearled ears, which were constantly in motion, its
fantastic gambols, had, I confess, a share of my admiration. As soon as the morning dawned, I escaped from
my mother's bed to visit my favourite, and carry it a
green leaf or two. There it sat, and gravely ate the
leaves, casting upon me protracted glances, which I
thought full of affection; then, erecting itself on its
hind paws, it turned to the sun its little snow-white
belly, and sleeked its fine whiskers with marvellous
dexterity.

"Nevertheless, slander was busy in its detraction; its face was too small, said its enemies, and it was very gluttonous. To-day, I might subscribe to these assertions; but at seven years of age I fought for the honour of my rabbit! Alas! there was no need to make it the subject of dispute, it lived so short a time. One Sunday, my mother having set out for the town with my sister and eldest brother, we were wandering—we, the little ones—in the enclosure, when a sudden report broke over our heads. A strange cry, like an infant's first moan, followed it close at hand. My rabbit had been wounded by a flash of fire. The unfortunate beast had transgressed beyond the vineyard-hedge, and a neighbour, having nothing better to do, had amused himself with shooting at it.

"I was in time to see it rise up, bleeding. So great was my grief that I almost choked, utterly unable to sob out a single word. But for my father, who received me in his arms, and by gentle words gave my full heart relief, I should have fainted. My limbs yielded under me. Pardon the tears which this recollection still calls forth.

"For the first time, and in early youth, I had a revelation of death, abandonment, desolation. The house, the garden, appeared to me empty and bare. Do not laugh: my grief was bitter, and all the deeper because concentrated in myself.

"Thenceforth, having learned the meaning of death, I began to watch my father with wistful eyes. I saw, not without terror, that his face was very pale and his hair white. He would quit us; he would go

'whither the village-bell summoned him,' to use his
oft-repeated phrase. I had not the strength to conceal
my thoughts. Sometimes I flung my arms around his
neck, exclaiming: 'Papa, do not die! oh, never die!'
He embraced me, without replying; but his fine large
black eyes were troubled as they gazed on me.

"I was attached to him by a thousand ties, by a
thousand intimate relations. I was the daughter of
his mature age, of his shattered health, of his affections.
I had not that happy equilibrium which his other children derived from my mother. My father was transmitted in me (*passé en moi*). He said so himself:
'How I feel that thou art my daughter!'

"Years and life's trials had deprived him of nothing;
to his last hour he retained the vivacity, the aspirations, and even the charm of youth. Every one felt
it without being able to account for it, and all flocked
around him of their own accord—women, children, men.
I still see him in his little study, seated before his
small black table, relating his Odyssey, his long jour-
neys in America, his life in the colonies; one never
grew weary of his stories. A maiden of twenty years,
in the last stage of a pulmonary disease, heard him
shortly before her end: she would fain have listened
to him always; implored him to visit her, for while he
was discoursing she forgot her sufferings and her decay,
even the approach of death.

"This charm I speak of was not that of a clever
talker only; it was due to the great goodness so
plainly visible in him. The trials, the life of adventure and misfortune, which harden so many hearts,

had, on the contrary, but softened his.   No man in
this generation—a generation so much agitated, tossed
to and fro by so many waves — had undergone such
painful experiences.   His father, an Auvergnat, the
principal of a college, then *juge consulaire* in our
most southern city, and finally summoned to the
Assembly of Notables in '88, had all the hard austerity
of his country and his functions, of the school and the
tribunals.   The education of that era was cruel, a perpetual chastisement ; the more wit, the more character,
the more strength, the more did this education tend to
shatter them, to break them down.   My father, of a
delicate and tender nature, could never have survived
it, and only escaped by flying to America, where one
of his brothers had previously established himself.   A
change of linen was his only fortune, except his youth,
his confidence, his golden dreams of freedom.   Thenceforth he always cherished a peculiar tenderness for that
land of liberty ; he often revisited it, and earnestly
wished to die there.

"Called by the needs of business to St. Domingo, he
was present in that island at the great crisis of the reign
of Toussaint L'Ouverture.   This truly extraordinary
man, who up to his fiftieth year had been a slave, who
comprehended and foresaw everything, did not know
how to write, or to give expression to his ideas.   His
genius succeeded better in great actions than in fine
speeches.   He lacked a hand, a pen, and more—the
young bold heart which shall teach the hero the heroic
language, the words in harmony with the moment and
the situation.   Toussaint, at his age, could only utter

this noble appeal: 'The First of the Blacks to the First of the Whites!' * Permit me to doubt if it were his. At least, if he conceived it, it was my father who gave expression to the idea.

"He loved my father warmly; he perceived his frankness, and he trusted him—he, so profoundly mistrustful, dumb with his long slavery, and secret as the tomb! But who can die without having one day unlocked his heart? It was my father's misfortune that at certain moments Toussaint broke his silence, and made him the confidant of dangerous mysteries. Thenceforth, all was over; he became afraid of the young man, and felt himself dependent upon him—a new servitude, which could only end with my father's death. Toussaint threw him into prison, and then, with a fresh access of fear, would have sacrificed him. Fortunately, the prisoner was guarded by gratitude; he had been bountiful to many of the blacks; a negress whom he had protected, warned him of his peril, and assisted him to escape from it. All his life long he sought that woman, to show his gratitude towards her; he did not discover her until some fourteen years afterwards, on his last voyage; she was then living in the United States.

"To return: though out of prison, he was not saved. Wandering astray in the forest, at night, without a guide, he had cause to dread the Maroons, those implacable enemies of the whites, who would have killed him, in ignorance that they were murdering the best

* It was with this exordium Toussaint commenced his appeal to Napoleon Bonaparte.

friend of their race. Fortune is the boon of youth;
he escaped every danger. Having discovered a good
horse, whenever the blacks issued from their hiding-
places, one touch of the spear, a wave of the hat, a
cry: 'Advanced guard of General Toussaint!' and this
was enough. At that formidable name all took to
flight, and disappeared as if by enchantment.

"Such was the tenderness of my father's soul, that
he did not withdraw his regard from the great man
who had misunderstood him. When, at a later period,
he saw him in France, abandoned by everybody, a
wretched prisoner in a fort of the Jura, where he
perished of cold and misery,* he alone was faithful to
him. Despite his errors, despite the deeds of violence
inseparable from the grand and terrible part which that
man had played, he revered in him the daring pioneer
of a race, the creator of a world. He corresponded
with him until his death, and afterwards with his
family.

"A singular chance ordained that my father should
be engaged in the isle of Elba when the First of the
Whites, dethroned in his turn, arrived to take possession of his miniature kingdom. Heart and imagination, my father fell captive to this wonderful romance.
An American, and imbued with Republican ideas, he
became on this occasion, and for the second time, the
courtier of misfortune. He was the most intimate of

---

* Napoleon's treatment of Toussaint L'Ouverture is one of the
darkest spots on his fame. He flung this son of the Tropics into a
dungeon among the icy fastnesses of the Alps, where he died, slain by
cold and undeserved ill-treatment, on the 27th of April 1803.—*Translator.*

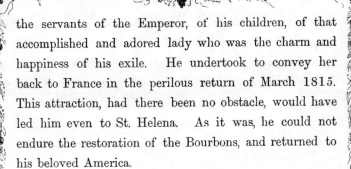

the servants of the Emperor, of his children, of that accomplished and adored lady who was the charm and happiness of his exile. He undertook to convey her back to France in the perilous return of March 1815. This attraction, had there been no obstacle, would have led him even to St. Helena. As it was, he could not endure the restoration of the Bourbons, and returned to his beloved America.

"The New World was not ungrateful, and made the happiness of his life. He had resigned every official capacity in order to abandon himself wholly to the more independent career of tuition. He taught in Louisiana. That colonial France, isolated, sundered by the events of her mother-land's history, and mingling so many diverse elements of population, breathes ever the breath of France. Among my father's pupils was an orphan, of English and German extraction. She came to him when very young, to learn the first elements of knowledge; she grew under his hands, and loved him more and more; she found a second family, a second father; she sympathized with the paternal heart, with a charm of youthful vivacity which our French of the south preserve in their mature age. She had but three faults: wealth, beauty, extreme youth—for she was at least thirty years younger than my father; but neither of them perceived it, and they never reminded themselves of it. My mother has been inconsolable for my father's death, and has ever since worn mourning.

"My mother longed to see France, and my father, in his pride of her, was delighted to show to the Old World the brilliant flower he had gathered in the New.

But anxious as he was to maintain this young Creole lady in the position and with the fortune which she had always enjoyed, he would not embark until he had accomplished, with her consent, a religious and holy act. This was the manumission of his slaves—of those, at least, above the age of twenty-one; the young, whom he was prevented by the American law from setting free, received from him their future liberty, and, on attaining their majority, were to rejoin their parents. He never lost sight of them. They were always before his eyes; he knew their names, their ages, and their appointed hour of liberty. In his French home, he took note of these epochs, and would say, with a glow of happiness, 'To-day, such an one becomes free!'

"See my father now in his native country, happy in a residence near his birth-place—building, planting, bringing up his family, the centre of a young world in which everything sprung from him: the house, the garden, were his creation; even his wife, whom he had reared and trained, and whom everybody thought to be his daughter. My mother was so young that her eldest daughter seemed to be her sister. Five other children followed, almost in as many successive years, promptly enwreathing my father with a living garland, which was his special pride. Few families exhibited a greater variety of tastes and temperaments; the two worlds were distinctly represented in ours: the French of the south with the sparkling vivacity of Languedoc—the grave colonists of Louisiana marked from their birth with the phlegmatic idiosyncrasies of the American character.

"It was ordered, however, that, with the exception of the eldest, who was already my mother's companion and shared with her the management of the household, the five youngest should receive their education in common from one master—my father. Notwithstanding his age, he undertook the duties of preceptor and schoolmaster. He gave up to us his whole day, from six in the morning until six in the evening. He reserved for his correspondence, his favourite studies, only the first hours of morning, or, more truly speaking, the last hours of night. Retiring to rest very early, he rose every day at three o'clock, without taking any heed of his pulmonary weakness. First of all, he threw wide his door, and there, before the stars or the dawn, according to the season, he blessed God; and God also blessed that venerable head, silvered by the experiences of life, not by the passions of humanity. In summer time, after his devotions, he took a short walk in the garden, and watched the insects and the plants awake. His knowledge of them was wonderful; and very often, after breakfast, taking me by the hand, he would describe the nature of each flower, would point out where each little animal that he had surprised at dawn took refuge. One of these was a snake, which the sight of my father did not in the least disconcert; each time that he seated himself near its domicile, it never failed to put forth its head and peer at him curiously. He alone knew that it was there, and he told none but me of its retirement; it remained a secret between us.

"In those morning-hours everything he met with

became a fertile text for his religious effusions. Without formal phrases, and inspired by true feeling, he spoke to me of the goodness of God, for whom there is neither great nor small, but all are brothers in His eyes, and all are equals.

"Associated with my brothers in their labours, I also took a part in those of my mother and my sister. When I put aside my grammar and arithmetic, it was to take up the needle.

"Happily for me, our life, naturally blending with that of the fields, was, whether we willed it or not, frequently varied by charming incidents which broke the chains of habit. Study has commenced; we apply ourselves with eagerness to our books; but what now? See, a storm is coming! the hay will be spoiled. Quick, we must gather it in! Everybody sets to work; the very children hasten thither; study is adjourned; we toil courageously, and the day goes by. It is a pity, for the rain does not fall; the storm has lingered on the Bordeaux side; it will come to-morrow.

"At harvest-time we frequently diverted ourselves with gleaning. In those grand moments of fruition, at once a labour and a festival, all sedentary application is impossible; one's thoughts are in the fields. We were constantly escaping out-of-doors, with the lark's swiftness; we disappeared among the furrows— we little ones concealed by the tall corn, hidden among the forest of ripe ears.

"It was well understood that during the vintage there was no time to think of study: much needed

labourers, we lived among the vines; it was our right.
But before the grape ripened, we had numerous other
vintages, those of the fruit-trees — cherries, apricots,
peaches. Even at a later period, the apples and the
pears imposed upon us new and severe labours, in
which it was a matter of conscience that our hands
should be employed. And thus, even in winter, these
necessities returned—to act, to laugh, and to do nothing.
The last tasks, occurring in mid-November, were perhaps
the most delightful; a light mist then enfolded everything; I have seen nothing like it elsewhere; it was a
dream, an enchantment. All objects were transfigured
under the wavy folds of the vast pearl-gray canopy
which, at the breath of the warm autumn, lovingly
alighted hither and thither, like a farewell kiss.

"The dignified hospitality of my mother, my father's
charm of manner and piquant conversation, drew upon
us also the unforeseen distractions of visitors from the
town, constraining suspensions of our studies, at which
we did not weep. But the great and unceasing visit
was from the poor, who well knew the house and the
hand inexhaustibly opened by charity. All partici-
pated in its benefits, even the very animals; and it
was a curious and diverting thing to see the dogs of
the neighbourhood, patiently, silently seated on their
hind legs, waiting until my father should raise his
eyes from his book: they felt assured that he would
not resist the mute eloquence of their prayer. My
mother, more reasonable, was inclined to drive away
these indiscreet guests who came at their own invitation.
My father felt that he was wrong, and yet he never

failed to throw them stealthily some fragments, which sent them away satisfied.

"This they knew perfectly well. One day, a new guest, lean, bristling, unprepossessing, something between a dog and a wolf, arrived; he was, in fact, a half-breed of the two species, born in the forests of the Gresigne. He was very ferocious, very irascible, and bore much too close a resemblance to his wolfish mother. But, besides this, he was intelligent, and gifted with a very keen instinct. From the first he gave himself wholly up to my father, and neither words nor rough usage could induce him to quit his side. For us he had but little love; and we repaid him in kind, seizing every opportunity of playing him a hundred tricks. He ground and gnashed his teeth, though, out of regard for my father, he abstained from devouring us. To the poor he was furious, implacable, very dangerous; which decided us on suffering him to be lost. But there was no such chance. He always came back again. His new masters would chain him to a post; chains and post, he carried them all off, and brought them into our house. It was too much for my father; he would never forsake him.

"But the cats enjoyed even more of his good graces than the dogs. This was due to his early education, to the cruel years spent at college; his brother and himself, beaten and repulsed, between the harshness of their home and the severities of their school, had found a consolation in a couple of cats. This predilection was transmitted to his family—each of us, in childhood, possessed our cat. The gathering at the fireside was

a beautiful spectacle; all the grimalkins, in furred
dignity, sitting majestically under the chairs of their
young masters.   One alone was missing from the
circle—a poor wretch, too ugly to figure among the
others; he knew his unworthiness, and held himself
aloof, in a wild timidity which nothing was able to
conquer.   As in every assembly (such is the piteous
malignity of our nature!) there must be a butt, a scape-
goat, who receives all the blows, he, in ours, filled this
unthankful rôle.   If there were no blows, at least there
were abundant mockeries: we named him Moquo.   Weak,
and scantily provided with fur, he stood in more need
than the others of the genial hearth; but we children
filled him with fear: even his comrades, better clothed
in their warm ermine, appeared to esteem him but
lightly, and to look at him askant.   Of course, therefore, my father turned to him, and fondled him; the
grateful animal lay down under that beloved hand,
and gained confidence.   Wrapped up in his coat, and
revived by its warmth, he would frequently be brought,
unseen, to the fireside.   We quickly caught sight of him;
and if he showed a hair, or the tip of an ear, our laughter
and our glances threatened him, in spite of my father.
I can still see that shadow gathering itself up—*melting*, so to speak—in its protector's bosom, closing its
eyes, annihilating itself, well content to see nothing.

   "All that I have read of the Hindus, and their
tenderness for nature, reminds me of my father.   He
was a Brahmin.   More even than the Brahmins did
he love every living thing.   He had lived in a time
of blood and war—he had been an eye-witness of the

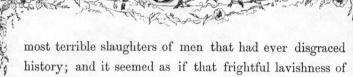

most terrible slaughters of men that had ever disgraced history; and it seemed as if that frightful lavishness of the irrecoverable good, which is life, had given him a respect for *all* life, an insurmountable aversion to all destruction.

"This had in time arrived at such an extreme, that he would have willingly lived upon vegetable food alone. He would have no viands of blood; they excited his horror. A morsel of chicken, or, more often, an egg or two, served for his dinner. And frequently he dined standing.

"Such a regimen, however, could not strengthen him. Nor did he economize his strength, expending it largely in lessons, in conversations, and in the habitual overflow of a too benevolent heart, which lived in all things, interested itself in all. Age came, and with it anxieties: family anxieties? no, but from jealous neighbours or unfaithful debtors. The crisis of the American banks dealt a severe blow to his fortune. He came to the extreme resolution, in spite of his ill health and his years, of once more visiting America, in the belief that his personal activity and his industry might re-establish affairs, and secure the fortune of his wife and children.

"This departure was terrible. It was preceded for me by another blow. I had quitted the mansion and the country; I had entered a boarding-school in the town. Cruel servitude, which deprived me of all that made my life—of air and respiration! Everywhere, walls! I should have died, but for the frequent visits of my mother, and the rarer visits of my father, to which I

looked forward with a delirious impatience that perhaps love has never known. But now that my father
himself was leaving us — heaven, earth, everything
seemed undone. With whatever hope of reunion he
might endeavour to cheer me, an internal voice, distinct and terrible, such as one hears in great trials, told
me that he would return no more.

"The house was sold, and the plantations laid out
by our hands, the trees which belonged to the family,
were abandoned. Our animals were plainly inconsolable
at my father's departure. The dog—I forget for how
many successive days—seated himself on the road which
he had taken at his departure, howled, and returned.
The most disinherited of all, the cat Moquo, no longer
confided in any person, though he still came to regard
with furtive glances the empty place. Then he took
his resolution, and fled to the woods, from which we
could never call him back; he resumed his early life,
miserable and savage.

"And I, too, I quitted the paternal roof, the hearth
of my young years, with a heart for ever wounded.
My mother, my sister, my brothers, the sweet friend-
ships of infancy, disappeared behind me. I entered
upon a life of trial and isolation. At Bayonne, however, where I first resided, the sea of Biarritz spoke to
me of my father; the waves which break on its shore,
from America to Europe, repeated the story of his death;
the snow-white ocean birds seemed to say, 'We have
seen him.'

"What remained to me? My climate, my birth-
land, my language. But even these I lost. I was

compelled to go to the North, to an unknown tongue
and a hostile sky, where the earth for half a year
wears mourning weeds.   During these long seasons of
frost, my failing health extinguishing imagination, I
could scarcely re-create for myself my ideal South.   A
dog might have somewhat consoled me: in default, I
made two little friends, who resembled, I fancied, my
mother's turtle-doves.   They knew me, loved me,
sported by my fireside; I gave to them the summer
which my heart had not.

"Seriously affected, I fell very ill, and thought I
should soon touch the other shore.   However studious
and tender towards me might be the hospitality of the
stranger, it was needful I should return to France.
It was long before carefulness of affection, and a
marriage in which I found again a father's heart and
arms, could restore my health.   I had seen death
from so near a view-point—let us rather say, I had
entered so far upon it—that nature herself, living
nature, that first love and rapture of my young years,
had for a long time little hold upon me, and she alone
had any.   Nothing had supplied her place.   History,
and the recital of the pathetic stirring human drama,
moved me but lightly; nothing seized firmly on my
mind but the unchangeable, God and Nature.

"Nature is immovable and yet mobile; that is her
eternal charm.   Her unwearied activity, her ever-
shifting phantasmagoria, do not weary, do not disturb;
this harmonious motion bears in itself a profound
repose.

"I was recalled to her by the flowers—by the cares

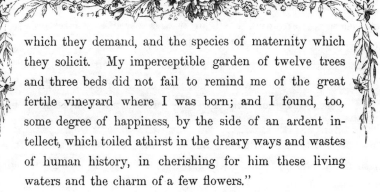

which they demand, and the species of maternity which
they solicit. My imperceptible garden of twelve trees
and three beds did not fail to remind me of the great
fertile vineyard where I was born; and I found, too,
some degree of happiness, by the side of an ardent intellect, which toiled athirst in the dreary ways and wastes
of human history, in cherishing for him these living
waters and the charm of a few flowers."

I resume.

See me now torn from the city by this loving inquietude, by my fears for an invalid whom it was essential to restore to the conditions of her early life and the free air of the country. I quitted Paris, my city, which I had never left before; that city which comprises the three worlds; that cradle of Art and Thought.

I returned there daily for my duties and occupations; but I hastened to get quit of it. Its noise, its distant hum, the ebb and flow of abortive revolutions, impelled me to wander afar. It was with much pleasure that, in the spring of 1852, I broke through all the ties of old habits; I closed my library with a bitter joy, I put under lock and key my books, the companions of my life, which had assuredly thought to hold me bound for ever. I travelled so long as earth supported me, and only halted at Nantes, close to the sea, on a hill which overlooks the yellow streams of Brittany as they flow onward to mingle, in the Loire, with the gray waters of La Vendée.

We established ourselves in a large country mansion, completely isolated, in the midst of the constant rains with which our western fields are inundated at this season. At such a distance from the ocean, one does not feel its briny influence; the rains are tempests of fresh water. The house, in the Louis Quinze style, had been uninhabited for a considerable period, and at first sight seemed a little gloomy. Situated on elevated ground, it was rendered not the less sombre by thick hedges on the one side, on the other by tall trees and by an untold number of unpruned cherry-trees. The whole, cn a greensward, which the undrained waters preserved, even in summer, in a beautifully fresh condition.

I adore neglected gardens, and this one reminded me of the great abandoned vineyards of the Italian villas; but it possessed, what these villas lack, a charming medley of vegetables and plants of a thousand different species—all the herbs of the St. John, and each herb tall and vigorous. The forest of cherry-trees, bending under their burden of scarlet fruit, gave also the idea of inexhaustible abundance.

It was not the sweet austerity (*soave austero*) of Italy; it was a soft and overflowing profusion, under a warm, mild, and moist sky.

Nothing appeared in sight, though a large town was close at hand, and a little river, the Erdre, wound under the hill, and from

thence dragged itself towards the Loire. But this vegetable prodigality, this virgin forest of fruit trees, completely shut in the view. For a prospect, one must mount into a species of turret, whence the landscape began to reveal itself in a certain grandeur, with its woods and its meadows, its distant monuments, its towers. Even from this observatory the view was still limited, the city appearing very imperfectly, and not allowing you to catch sight of its mighty river, its islands, its stir of commerce and navigation. A few paces from its great harbour, of whose existence there was no sign, one might believe oneself in a desert, in the *landes* of Brittany, or the clearings of La Vendée.

Two things were of a lofty character, and detached them-

selves from this sombre orchard.   Penetrating the ancient hedges
and chestnut-alleys, you found yourself in a nook of barren argil-
laceous soil, where, among thyme-laurels and other strong, rude trees,
rose an enormous cedar, a veritable leafy cathedral, of such stature
that a cypress already grown very tall was choked by it, and lost.
This cedar, bare and stripped below, was living and vigorous where
it received the light; its immense arms, at thirty feet from the
ground, clothed themselves with strange and pointed leaves; then
the canopy thickened; the trunk attained an elevation of eighty feet.
You saw, about three leagues distant, the fields opposite the banks

of the Sèvre and the woods of La Vendée.   Our home, low and
sheltered on the side of this giant, was not less distinguished by it

throughout an immense circuit, and perhaps owed to it its name, the High Forest.

At the other end of the enclosure, from a deep sheet of water, rose a small ascent, crowned with a garland of pines. These fine trees, incessantly beaten by the sea-breezes, and shaken by the adverse winds which follow the currents of the great river and its two tributaries, groaned in the struggle, and day and night filled the profound silence of the place with a melancholy harmony. At times, you might have thought yourself by the sea; they so imitated the noise of the waves, of the ebbing and flowing tide.

By degrees, as the season became a little drier, this sojourn exhibited itself to me in its real character; serious, indeed, but more varied than one would have supposed at the first glance, and beautiful with a touching beauty which went home to the soul. Austere, as became the gate of Brittany, it had all the luxuriant verdure of the Vendean coast.

I could have thought, when I saw the pomegranates blooming in the open air, robust and loaded with flowers, that I was in the south. The magnolia, no dwarf, as we see it elsewhere, but splendid and magnificent, and full-grown, like a great tree, perfumed all my garden with its huge white blossoms, which contain in their thick chalices an abundance of I know not what kind of oil, an oil sweet and penetrating, whose odour follows you everywhere; you are enveloped in it.

We found ourselves this time in possession of a true garden, a large establishment, a thousand domestic occupations with which we had previously dispensed. A wild Breton girl rendered help only in the coarser tasks. Save one weekly journey to the town, we were very lonely, but in an extremely busy solitude; rising very early in the morning, at the first awakening of the birds, and even before the day. It is true that we retired to rest at a good hour, and almost at the same time as the birds.

This profusion of fruits, vegetables, and plants of every kind, enabled us to keep numerous domestic animals: only the difficulty was, that nourishing them, knowing each of them, and well-known by them, we could not make up our minds to eat them. We planted, and here we met with quite a distinct kind of inconvenience—our plantations were nearly always devoured beforehand.

This earth, fertile in vegetables, was equally or more prolific of destructive animals ; enormous capacious snails, devouring insects. In the morning we collected a great tubful of snails. The next day you would never have thought so. There still seemed to be the full complement.

Our hens did their best. But how much more effective would have been the skilful and prudent stork, the admirable scavenger of Holland and all marshy districts, which some Western lands ought at all costs to adopt. Everybody knows the affectionate respect in which this excellent bird is held by the Dutch. In their markets you may see him standing peacefully on one foot, dreaming in the midst of the crowd, and feeling as safe as in the heart of the deepest deserts. It is a fantastic but well-assured fact, that the Dutch peasant who has had the misfortune to wound his stork and to break his leg, provides him with one of wood.

To return: our residence near Nantes would have possessed an infinite charm for a less absorbed mind. This beautiful spot, this great liberty of work, this solitude, so sweet in such society, formed a rare harmony, such as one but seldom meets with in life. Its sweetness contrasted strongly with the thoughts of the present, with the gloomy

past which then occupied my pen.   I was writing of '93.   Its heroic
primeval history enveloped, possessed, shall I say consumed, me.   All
the elements of happiness which surrounded me, which I sacrificed to
work, adjourning them for a time that, according to all appearances,

might never be mine, I regretted daily, and incessantly cast back
upon them a look of sorrow.   It was a daily battle of affection and
nature, against the sombre thoughts of the human world.

   That battle for me will be always a powerful *souvenir*.   The
scene has remained sacred in my thought.   Elsewhere it no longer
exists.   The house is destroyed—another built on its site.   And it
is for this reason that I have dallied here a little.   My cedar, however, has survived ; a notable thing, for architects now-a-days hate
trees.

   When, however, I drew near the end of my task, some glimpses
of light enlivened the wild darkness.   My sorrows were less keen,
when I felt sure that I should thenceforth enjoy this memorial of a
cruel but fertile experience.   Once more I began to hear the voices

of solitude, and more plainly I believe than at any other age, but slowly and with unaccustomed ear, like one who shall have been some time dead, and have returned from the other world.

In my youth, before I was taken captive by this implacable History, I had sympathized with nature, but with a blind warmth, with a heart less tender than ardent. 'At a later period, when residing in the suburb of Paris, I had again felt that emotion of love. I watched with interest my sickly flowers in that arid soil, so sensible every evening of the joy of refreshing waterings, so plainly grateful. How much more at Nantes, surrounded by a nature ever powerful and prolific, seeing the herbage shoot upward hour after hour, and all animal life multiplying around me, ought I not, I too, to expand and revive with this new sentiment!

If there were aught that could have re-inspired my mind and broken the sombre spell that lay upon it, it would have been a book which we frequently read in the evening, the "Birds of France," by Toussenel, a charming and felicitous transition from the thought of country to that of nature.

So long as France exists, his Lark and his Redbreast, his Bullfinch, his Swallow, will be incessantly read, re-read, re-told. And if there were no longer a France, in its ingenious pages we should re-discover

all which it owned of good, the true breath of that country, the Gallic sense, the French *esprit*, the very soul of our fatherland.

The formulæ of a system which it bears, however, very lightly, its forced comparisons (which sometimes make us think of those too *spirituel* animals of Granville), do not prevent the French genius, gay, good, serene, and courageous, young as an April sun, from illuminating the entire book. It possesses numerous passages enlivened with the joyousness, the elasticity, the gushing song of the lark in the first day of spring.

Add, too, a circumstance of great beauty, which is not connected with youth. The author, a child of the Meuse and of a land of hunters, himself in his early years an ardent and impassioned sportsman, appears altered in character by his book. He wavers visibly between the first habits of slaughterous youth, and his new sentiment, his tenderness for those pathetic lives which he unveils—for these souls, these beings recognized by his soul. I dare to say that henceforth he will never again hunt without remorse. The father and the second creator of this world of love and innocence, he will find interposed between them and him a barrier of compassion. And what barrier? His own work, the book in which he gives them life.

I had scarcely begun my book, when it became necessary for me to leave Nantes. I, too, was ill. The dampness of the climate, the hard continuous labour, and still more keenly, without doubt, the conflict of my thoughts, seemed to have struck home to that vital nerve of which nothing had ever before taken hold. The road which our swallows tracked for us, we followed; we proceeded southward. We fixed our transitory nest in a fold of the Apennines, two leagues from Genoa.

An admirable situation, a secure and well-defended shelter, which, in the variable climate of that coast, enjoys the astonishing boon of an equable temperature. Although one could not entirely dispense with fires, the winter sun, warm in January, encouraged the lizard and the invalid to think it was spring. Shall I confess it, however? These oranges, these citrons, harmonizing in their changeless foliage with the changeless blue of heaven were not without monotony. Animated life was very rare. There were few or no small birds; no sea birds. The fish, limited in numbers, did not fill with life those

translucent waters.   My glance pierced them to a great depth, and
saw nothing but solitude, and the white and black rocks which form
the bed of that gulf of marble.

The littoral, exceedingly narrow, is nothing but a small cornice, an
extremely confined border, a mere eyebrow (*sourcil*) of the mountains,
as the Latins would have said.   To ascend its steps, and overlook
the gulf is, even for the most robust, a violent gymnastic effort.   My
sole promenade was a little quay, or rather a rugged circular road,
which wound, with a breadth of about three feet, between ancient
garden walls, rocks, and precipices.

Deep was the silence, sparkling the sea, but all lonesome and
monotonous, except for the passage of a few distant barks.   Work
was prohibited to me; for the first time for thirty years, I was separated
from my pen, and had escaped from that paper and ink existence in
which I had previously lived.   This pause, which I thought so

barren, in reality proved to me very fertile. I watched, I observed. Unknown voices awoke within me.

At some distance from Genoa, and the excellent friends whom we knew there, our only society was the small people of the lizards, which run over the rocks, played, and slumbered in the sun. Charming, innocent animals, which every noon, when we dined, and the quay was absolutely deserted, amused me with their vivacious and graceful evolutions. At the outset my presence had appeared to disquiet them ; but a week had not passed before all, even the youngest, knew me, and knew they had nothing to fear from the peaceful dreamer.

Such the animal, and such the man. The abstemious life of my lizards, for which a fly was an ample banquet, differed in nothing from that of the *povera gente* of the coast. Many lived wholly on herbs. But herbs were not abundant in the barren and gaunt mountain. The destitution of the country exceeded all belief. I was not grieved at daring it, at finding myself sympathizing with the woes of Italy, my glorious nurse, who has nourished France, and me more than any Frenchman.

A nurse ? That was she ever, so far as was possible in her poverty of resources, in the poverty of nature to which my health reduced me. Incapable of food, I still received from her the only nourishment which I could support, the vivifying air and the light—the sun, which frequently permitted us, in one of the severest winters of the century, to keep the windows open in January.

In the lazy, lizard-like life which I lived upon that shore, I wholly occupied myself with the surrounding country, with the apparent antiquity of the Apennines and the mountains which girdle the Mediterranean. Is there then no remedy ? Or rather, in their leafless declivities shall we not discover the fountains which may renew their life ? Such was the idea which absorbed me. I no longer thought of my illness ; I troubled myself no more about recovering. I had made what is truly great progress for an invalid : I had forgotten myself. My business henceforward was to resuscitate that mighty patient, the Apennines. And as by degrees I became aware that the case was not hopeless—that the waters were hidden, not lost—that by their discovery we might restore vegetable life, and eventually animal life,—I felt myself much stronger, refreshed, renewed. For each spring that revealed itself, I grew less athirst; I felt its waters rise within my soul.

Ever fertile is Italy. She proved so to me through her very barrenness and poverty. The ruggedness of the bald Apennines, the lean Ligurian coast, did but the more awaken, by contrast, the recollection of that genial nature which cherishes the luxuriant richness of our western France. I missed the animal life; I felt its absence. From the mute foliage of sombre orange-gardens I demanded the woodland birds. For the first time I perceived the seriousness of human existence when it is no longer surrounded by the grand society of innocent beings whose movements, voices, and sports are, so to speak, the smile of creation.

A revolution took place in me which I shall, perhaps, some day relate. I returned, with all the strength of my ailing existence, to the thoughts which I had uttered, in 1846, in my book of "The People," to that City of God where the humble and simple, peasants and artisans, the ignorant and unlettered, barbarians and savages, children, and those other children, too, which we call animals, are all citizens under different titles, have all their privileges and their laws, their places at the great civic banquet. "I protest, for my part, that if any one remains in the rear whom the City still rejects and does not shelter with her rights, I myself will not enter in, but will halt upon her threshold."

Thus, all natural history I had begun to regard as a branch of the political. Every living species came, each in its humble right, striking at the gate and demanding admittance to the bosom of Democracy. Why should their elder brothers repulse them beyond the pale of those laws which the universal Father harmonizes with the law of the world?

Such, then, was my renovation, this tardy new life (vita nuova), which led me, step by step, to the natural sciences. Italy, whose influence over my destiny has always been great, was its scene, its occasion, just as, thirty years before, it had lit for me, through Vico, the first spark of the historic fire.

Beloved and beneficent nurse! Because I had for one moment shared her sorrows, suffered, dreamed with her, she bestowed on me a priceless gift, worth more than all the diamonds of Golconda. What gift? A profound sympathy of spirit, a fruitful interchange of the most intimate ideas, a perfect home-harmony in the thought of Nature.

We arrived at this goal by two paths : I, by my love of the City, by the effort of completing it through an association of self with all other beings ; my wife, by religious feeling and by her filial reverence for the fatherhood of God.

Henceforth we were able, every evening, to enjoy a mutual feast.

I have already explained how this work, unknown to ourselves, grew rich, was rendered fruitful, was impelled forward, by our modest auxiliaries. They have almost always dictated it.

Our Parisian flowers prepared what our birds of Nantes accomplished. A certain nightingale of which I speak at the close of the book crowned the work.

These divers impressions blended and melted together, on our return to France, and especially here, in the presence of the ocean. At the promontory of La Hève, under the venerable elms which overshadow it, this revelation completed itself. The gulls, gannets, and guillemots of the coast, the small birds of the groves, could say nothing which was not understood. All things found an echo in our hearts, like so many internal voices.

The Pharos, the huge cliff, from three to four hundred feet in height,* which from so lofty an elevation overlooks the vast embouchure of the Seine, the Calvados, and the ocean, was the customary goal of our promenades, and our resting-point. We usually climbed to it by a deep covered road, full of freshness and shadow, which suddenly opened upon this immense lighthouse. Sometimes we ascended the

---

* There are two lights, of which the more elevated is 396 feet above the sea-level.— *Translator.*

colossal staircase which, without surprises, in the full sunlight, and
always facing the mighty sea, leads by three flights to the summit,
each flight covering upwards of a hundred feet.   You cannot accomplish this ascent at one breath ; at the second stage, you breathe, you
seat yourself for a few moments by the monument which the widow
of one of France's greatest soldiers has raised to his memory, in the
hope that its pyramid might prove a beacon to the mariner, and
guard him from shipwreck.

This cliff, of a very sandy soil, loses a little every winter.*   It is
not, however, the sea which gnaws at it ; the heavy rains wash it
away, carrying off the débris, which, at first bare and shapeless, bear
eloquent witness to their downfall.   But tender and gracious Nature
does not long suffer this.   She speedily attires them, bestows upon
them greensward, herbs, shrubs, briers, which in due time become
miniature oases on the declivity, Liliput landscapes suspended on
the vast cliff, consoling its gloomy barrenness with their sweet youth.

Thus the Beautiful and the Sublime here embrace, a thing of rarity.

---

* La Hève is the ancient Caletorum Promontorium, and situated about three miles north-
west of Havre.—*Translator*

The storm-beaten mountain relates to you the *epopea* of earth, its rude dramatic history, and shows its bones in evidence of its truth. But these young children of chance, who spring up on its arid flank, prove that she is still fertile, that her débris contain the elements of a new organization, that all death is a life begun.

So these ruins have never caused us any sadness. We have conversed among them freely of destiny, providence, death, the life to come. I, to whom age and toil have given a right to die,—she, whose brow is already bent by the trials of infancy and a wisdom beyond her years,—we have not lived the less for a grand inspiration of soul, for the rejuvenescent breath of that much-loved mother, Nature.*

Sprung from her at so great a distance from one another, so united in her to-day, we would fain have rendered eternal this rare moment of existence, and "have cast anchor on the island of time." And how could we better realize our dream than by this work of tenderness, of universal brotherhood, of adoption of all life !

My wife incessantly recalled me to it, enlarging my sentiments of individual tenderness by her facile, bright, emotional interpretation of the spirit of the country and the voices of solitude.

It was then, among other things, that I learned to understand those birds which, like the swallows, sing little, but talk much ; prattling of the fine weather, of the chase, of scanty or abundant food, of their approaching departure ; in fact, of all their affairs. I had listened to them at Nantes in October, at Turin in June. Their September *causeries* were more intelligible at La Hève. We translated them easily in all their fond vivacity, all their joyousness of youth and good-humour, free from ostentation or satire, in accord with the happy moderation of a bird so free and so wise, which appears not ungratefully to recognize that he has received from God a lot of the most signal felicity.

Alas ! even the swallow is not spared in that senseless warfare

---

* That the reader may feel the full force of this passage, I subjoin the original : " Nous n'en vivions pas moins d'un grand souffle d'âme, de la rajeunissante haleine de cette mère aimée, la Nature."

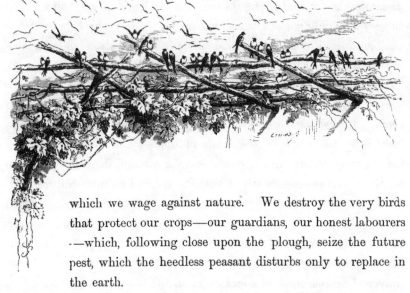

which we wage against nature. We destroy the very birds
that protect our crops—our guardians, our honest labourers
-—which, following close upon the plough, seize the future
pest, which the heedless peasant disturbs only to replace in
the earth.

Whole races, valuable and interesting, perish. Those lords of ocean,
those wild and sagacious creatures which Nature has endowed with
blood and milk—I speak of the cetacea—to how small a number are
they reduced! Many great quadrupeds have vanished from the globe.
Many animals of every kind, without utterly disappearing, have
recoiled before man; brutalized (*ensauvagés*) they fly, they lose their
natural arts, and relapse into barbarism. The heron, whose prudence
and address were remarked by Aristotle, is now, at least in
Europe, a misanthropical, narrow-minded, half-foolish creature. The
beaver, which, in America, in its peaceful solitudes, had become
a great architect and engineer, has grown discouraged;* to-day
it has scarcely the heart to excavate a burrow in the earth. The
hare, so gentle, so handsome, distinguished by its fur, its swiftness,
its wonderful delicacy of ear, will soon have passed away; the few
of its kind which remain are positively embruted. And yet the

---

* Compare the interesting descriptions of the huge dams erected by beavers across the
American rivers, in Milton and Cheadle's valuable narrative of travel, " The North-West
Passage by Land "—*Translator.*

poor animal is still docile and teachable : in careful hands it might be taught the things most antagonistic to its nature, even those which need a display of courage.*

These thoughts, which others have expressed in far better language, we cherished at heart. They had been our aliment, our habitual dream, over which we had brooded for two years, in Brittany, in Italy ; it is here that they have developed into— what shall I say—a book ? a living fruit ? At La Hève they appeared to us in their genial idea, that of the primitive alliance which God has ordained for all his creatures, of the love-bond which the universal mother has sealed between her children.

The winged order—the loftiest, the tenderest, the most sympathetic with man—is that which man now-a-days pursues most cruelly.

What is required for its protection ? To reveal the bird as a *soul*, to show that it is a *person*.

The Bird, then,—the Bird alone,—that is all my book ; but the Bird in all the variations of its destiny, as it accommodates itself to the thousand conditions of earth, to the thousand vocations of the winged life. Without any knowledge of the more or less ingenious systems of transformations, the heart gives oneness to its object ; it neither allows itself to be arrested by the external differences of species, nor by that death which seems to sever the thread. Death, rude and cruel, intervenes in this book, as in the full current of life, but as a passing accident only ; life does not the less continue.

The agents of death, the murdering species, so glorified by man, who recognizes in them his image, are here replaced very low in the hierarchy, remitted to the rank which is rightly theirs. They are the most deficient in the two special qualifications of the bird— nest-making and song. Sad instruments of the fatal passage, they appear in the midst of this book as the blind ministers of nature's hardest necessity.

But the lofty light of life—art in its earliest dawn—shines only

* The reader will hardly require to be reminded of the poet Cowper and his hares.— *Translator.*

in the smallest. With the small birds, unostentatious as they are, and modestly and seriously clad, art begins, and, on certain points, rises higher than the sphere of man. Far from equalling the nightingale, we have been unable to translate or to render the meaning of his sublime song.

The eagle, then, is in these pages dethroned; the nightingale reigns in his stead. In that moral *crescendo*, where the bird continuously advances in self-culture, the apex and the supreme point are naturally discovered, not in brutal strength, so easily overpassed by man, but in a puissance of art, of soul, and of aspiration which man has not attained, and which, beyond this world, transports him in a moment to the further spheres.

High justice and true, because it is clear-visioned and tender! Feeble on too many points, I doubt not, this book is strong in tenderness and faith. It is one, constant and faithful. Nothing makes it divaricate. Above death and its false divorce, through life and the   ks which disguise its unity, it flies, it loves to hover, from nest to nest, from egg to egg, from love to the love of God.

La Hève, near Havre, *September* 21, 1855.

Part First.

THE EGG.

THE EGG.

THE wise ignorance, the clear-seeing instinct of our forefathers gave utterance to this oracle: "Everything springs from the egg; it is the world's cradle."

Even our origin, but more especially the difference of our destiny, is due to the Mother. She acts and she foresees, she loves with a stronger or a weaker love, she is more or less maternal. The more she is so, the higher mounts her offspring; each degree in existence depends on the degree of her love.

What can the mother effect in the mobile existence of the fish? Nothing, but trust her birth to the ocean. What in the insect world, where she generally dies as soon as she has produced the egg? To obtain for it before dying a secure asylum, where it may come to light, and live.

In the case of the superior animal, the quadruped, where the

warm blood should surely stir up love, where the mother's womb is
so long the rest and home of her young, the cares of maternity are
also of minor import. The offspring is born fully formed, clothed
in all things like its parent ; and its food awaits it. And in many
species its education is accomplished without any further care on the
part of the mother than she bestowed when it grew in her bosom.

Far otherwise is the destiny of the bird. It would die if it
were not loved.

Loved ! Every mother loves, from the ocean to the stars. I
should rather say anxiously tended, surrounded by infinite affection,
enfolded in the warmth of the maternal magnetism.

Even in the egg, where you see it protected by a calcareous
shell, it feels so keenly the access of air, that every chilled point
in the egg is a limb or an organ the less for the future bird. Hence
the prolonged and disquieted labour of incubation, the self-inflicted
captivity, the motionlessness of the most mobile of beings. And all
this so very pitiful ! A stone pressed so long to the heart, to the
flesh—often the live flesh !

It is born, but born naked. While the baby-quadruped, even
from its first day of life, is clothed, and crawls, and already walks,
the young bird (especially in the higher species) lies motionless upon
its back, without the protection of any feathers. It is not only
while hatching it, but in anxiously rubbing it, that the mother maintains and stimulates warmth. The colt can readily suckle and
nourish itself ; the young bird must wait while the mother seeks,
selects, and prepares its food. She cannot leave it ; the father
must here supply her place ; behold the real, veritable family, faithfulness in love, and the first moral enlightenment.

I will say nothing here of a protracted, very peculiar, and very
hazardous education—that of flight. And nothing here of that of
song, so refined among the feathered artists. The quadruped soon
knows all that he will ever know : he gallops when born ; and if
he experiences an occasional fall, is it the same thing, tell me, to slide
without danger among the herbage, as to drop headlong from the skies?

Let us take the egg in our hands. This elliptical form, at once the easiest of comprehension, the most beautiful, and presenting the fewest salient points to external attack, gives one the idea of a complete miniature world, of a perfect harmony, from which nothing can be taken away, and to which nothing can be added. No inorganic matter adopts this perfect outline. I conceive that, under its apparent inertness, it holds a high mystery of life and a completed work of God.

What is it, and what should issue from it? I know not. But *she* knows well—yonder trembling creature who, with outstretched wings, embraces it and matures it with her warmth; she who, until now the free queen of the air, lived at her own wild will, but, suddenly fettered, sits motionless on that mute object which one would call a stone, and which as yet gives forth no sign of life.

Do not speak of blind instinct. Facts demonstrate how that clear-sighted instinct modifies itself according to surrounding conditions; in other words, how that rudimentary reason differs in its nature from the lofty human reason.

Yes; that mother knows and sees distinctly by means of the penetration and clairvoyance of love. Through the thick calcareous shell, where your rude hand perceives nothing, she feels by a delicate tact the mysterious being which she nourishes and forms. It is this feeling which sustains her during the arduous labour of incubation, during her protracted captivity. She sees it delicate and charming in its soft down of infancy, and she predicts with the vision of hope that it will be vigorous and bold, when, with outspread wings, it shall eye the sun and breast the storm.

Let us profit by these days. Let us hasten nothing. Let us contemplate at our leisure this delightful image of the maternal reverie—-of that second childbirth by which she completes the invisible object of her love—the unknown offspring of desire.

A delightful spectacle, but even more sublime than delightful. Let us be modest here. With us the mother loves that which stirs in her bosom—that which she touches, clasps, enfolds in assured possession; she loves the reality, certain, agitated and moving, which responds to her own movements. But this one loves the future and the unknown; her heart beats solitarily, and nothing as yet responds to its pulsations. Yet is not her love the less intense; she devotes herself and suffers; she will suffer unto death for her dream and her faith.

A faith powerful and efficacious! It produces a world, and one of the most wonderful of worlds. Speak not to me of suns, or the elementary chemistry of globes. The marvel of a humming-bird's egg transcends the wonders of the Milky Way.

Understand that this little point which to you seems imperceptible, is an entire ocean—the sea of milk where floats in embryo the well-beloved of heaven. It floats; fears no shipwreck; it is held suspended by the most delicate ligaments; it is saved from jar and shock. It swims all gently in the warm element, as it will swim hereafter in the atmosphere. A profound serenity, a perfect repose in the bosom of a nourishing habitation! And how superior to all suckling (*allaitement*)!

But see how, in this divine sleep, it has recognized its mother and her magnetic warmth. And it, too, begins to dream. Its dream is of motion; it imitates, it conforms to its mother; its first act, the act of an obscure love, is to resemble her.

" Knowest thou not that love transforms
Into itself whate'er it loves ? "

And as soon as it resembles her, it will seek to join her. It inclines, it presses more closely against the shell, which thenceforth is the sole barrier between it and its mother. Then, then she listens! Sometimes she is blessed by hearing already its first tender piping. It will remain a prisoner no longer. Grown daring, it will take its own part. It has a beak, and makes use of it. It strikes, it cracks, it cleaves its prison wall. It has feet, and brings them to its assistance. See now the work begun! Its reward is deliverance; it enters into liberty.

To tell the rapture, the agitation, the prodigious inquietude, the mother's many cares, is beyond our province here; of the difficulties of its education we have already spoken.

It is only through time and tenderness that the bird receives its initiation. Superior by its powers of flight, it is so much the more so through this, that it has had a home and has gained life through its mother; fed by her, and by its father emancipated, the freest of beings is the favourite of love.

If one wishes to admire the fertility of nature, the vigour of invention, the charming, and in a certain sense, the terrifying richness, which from one identical creation draws a million of opposite miracles, one should regard this egg, so exactly like another, and yet the source whence shall issue the innumerable tribes born to a life of wings on earth.

From the obscure unity it pours out, it expands, in countless and prodigiously divergent rays, those winged flames which you name birds, glowing with ardour and life, with colour and song. From the

burning hand of God escapes continuously that vast fan of astounding diversity, where everything shines, where everything sings, where everything floods me with harmony and light. Dazzled, I lower my eyes.

Melodious sparks of celestial fire, whither do ye not attain? For ye exists nor height nor distance; the heaven, the abyss, it is all one. What cloud, what watery deep is inaccessible to ye? Earth, in all its vast circuit, great as it is with its mountains, its seas, and its valleys, is wholly yours. I hear ye under the Equator, ardent as the arrows of the sun. I hear ye at the Pole, in the eternal lifeless silence, where the last tuft of moss has faded; the very bear sees ye afar, and slinks away growling. Ye, ye still remain; ye live, ye love, ye bear witness to God, ye reanimate death. In those terrestrial deserts your touching loves invest with an atmosphere of innocence what man has designated the barbarism of nature.

THE POLE—AQUATIC BIRDS.

THE POLE.

AQUATIC BIRDS.

THAT powerful fairy which endows man with most of his blessings and misfortunes, Imagination, sets herself to work to travestie nature for him in a hundred ways. In all things which exceed his energies or wound his sensations, in all the necessities which overrule the harmony of the world, he is tempted to see and to curse a maleficent will. One writer has made a book against the Alps; a poet has foolishly placed the throne of evil among those beneficent glaciers which are the reservoir of the waters of Europe, which pour forth its rivers and make its fertility. Others, still more absurdly, have vented their wrath upon the ices of the Pole, misunderstanding the magnificent economy of the globe, the majestic balance of those alternating currents which are the life of Ocean.   They have seen war and hate, and the malice of nature, in those regular and profoundly pacific movements of the universal Mother.

Such are the dreams of man.   Animals, however, do not share in these antipathies and idle terrors ; a twofold attraction, on the contrary, impels them yearly towards the Poles in innumerable legions.

Every year birds, fishes, gigantic cetaceans, hasten to people the seas and islands which surround the southern Pole.   ·Those wonderful seas ! so fertile, so full to overflowing of rudimentary life (in the zoophytic stage), of living fermentation, of viscous waters, of spawn, and superabundant embryos.

Both the Poles are for these innocent myriads, everywhere pursued by foes, the great, the happy rendezvous of love and peace. The whale,—that unfortunate fish, which has, however, like ourselves, sweet milk and hot blood,—that poor proscribed unfortunate which will soon have disappeared,—there again finds a refuge, and a pause for the sacred moments of maternity.   No races are of purer or gentler disposition, none more fraternal towards their kin, more tender towards their offspring.   Cruel ignorance of man !   How can he have slain without horror the walrus and the seal, which in so many points resemble himself ?

The giant-man of the old ocean, the whale—a being as gentle as man the dwarf is brutal—enjoys this advantage over him : sure of species whose fecundity is alarming, it can accomplish the mission of destruction which nature has ordained, without inflicting upon them any pain.   It has neither teeth nor saw ; none of those means of punishment with which the destroyers of the world are so abundantly provided.   Suddenly absorbed in the depths of this moving crucible, they lose themselves, they swoon away, they undergo instantaneously the transformations of its grand chemistry.   Most of the living matter on which the inhabitants of the Polar Seas support themselves—cetaceans, fishes, birds—have neither organism nor the means of suffering

Hence these tribes possess a character of innocence which moves us infinitely, fills us with sympathy, and also, we must confess, with envy. Thrice blessed, thrice fortunate that world where life renews and repairs itself without the cost of death—that world which is generally free from pain, which ever finds in its nourishing waters the sea of milk, has no need of cruelty, and still clings to Nature's kindly breast!

Before man's appearance, profound was the peace of these solitudes and their amphibious races. From the bear and the blue fox, the two tyrants of that region, they found an easy shelter in the ever-open bosom of the sea, their bountiful nurse.

When our mariners first landed there, their only difficulty was to pierce through the mass of curious and kindly-natured phocæ which came to gaze upon them. The penguins of Australian lands, the auks and razor-bills of the Arctic shores, peaceable and more active, made no movement. The wild geese, whose fine down, of incomparable softness, furnishes the much-prized eider, readily permitted the spoilers to approach and seize them with their hands.

The attitude of these novel creatures was the cause of pleasant mistakes on the part of our navigators. Those who from afar first saw the islands thronged with penguins, standing upright, in their costume of white and black, imagined them to be bands of children in white aprons! The stiffness of their small arms—one can scarcely call them wings in these rudimentary birds—their awkwardness on land, their difficulty of movement, prove that they belong to the ocean, where they swim with wonderful ease, and which is their natural and legitimate element. One might speak of them as its emancipated eldest sons, as ambitious fishes, candidates for the characters of birds, which had already progressed so far as to transform their fins into scaly pinions. The metamorphosis was not attended with complete success; powerless and clumsy as birds, they remain skilful and successful as fishes.

Or again, with their large feet attached so near to the body, with their neck short or poised on a great cylindrical trunk, with their flattened head, one might judge them to be near relations of their neighbours the seals, whose kindly nature they possess, but not their intelligence.

These eldest sons of nature, eye-witnesses of the ancient ages of transformation, appeared like so many strange hieroglyphics to those who first beheld them. With eyes mild, but sad and pale as the face of ocean, they seemed to regard man, the last-born of the planet, from the depths of their antiquity.

Levaillant found them in great numbers on a desert isle, not far from the Cape of Good Hope, where rose the tomb of a poor Danish mariner, a child of the Arctic Pole, whom Fate had led thither to die among the Austral wastes, and between whom and his fatherland the density of the globe intervened. Seals and penguins supplied him with a numerous society; the former prostrate and lying down; the latter standing erect, and mounting guard with dignity around the lonely grave: all melancholy, and responding to the moans of Ocean, which one might have imagined to be the wail of the dead.

Their winter station is the Cape. In that warm African exile they invest themselves with a good and solid coat of fat, which will be very useful defences for them against cold and hunger. When spring returns, a secret voice admonishes them that the tempestuous thaw has broken and rent the sharp crystalline ice; that the blissful Polar Seas, their country and their cradle, their sweet love-Eden, are open and calling upon them. Impatiently they set forth; with rapid wings they oar their way across five or six hundred leagues of sea, without other resting-place than occasional pieces of floating ice may, for a few moments, offer them. They arrive, and all is ready. A summer of thirty days' duration makes them happy.

With a grave happiness; with the happiness of discovering a profound tranquillity separating them from the sea where their sole aliment lies. The season of love and incubation is, therefore, a time of fasting and inquietude. The blue fox, their enemy, chases them into the desert. But union is strength. The mothers all incubate at one and the same time, and the legion of fathers watches around them, prepared to sacrifice themselves in their behalf. Let but the little one be hatched, and the serried ranks conduct it to the sea; it leaps into the waters, and is saved!

Stern, sad climates! Yet who would not love them, when he sees there the vast tenderness of nature, which impartially orders the home of man and the bird, the central source of love and devotion? From nature the Northern home receives a moral grace which that of the South rarely possesses; a sun shines there which is not the sun of the Equator, but far more gentle—that of the soul. There every creature is exalted, either by the very austerity of the climate or the urgency of peril.

The supreme effort in this world of the North, which is nowhere that of beauty, is to have discovered the Beautiful. This miracle springs from the mother's soul. Lapland has but one art, one solitary object of art—the cradle. "It is a charming object," says a lady who has visited those regions; "elegant and graceful, like a pretty little shoe lined with the soft fur of the white hare, more delicate than the feathers of the swan. Around the hood, where the infant's head is completely protected, warmly and softly sheltered, are hung festoons of coloured pearls, and tiny chains of copper or silver which clink incessantly, and whose jingling makes the young Laplander laugh."

O wonder of maternity! Through its influence the rudest woman becomes artistic, tenderly heedful. But the female is always heroic. It is one of the most affecting spectacles to see the bird of the eider— the eider-duck,—plucking its down from its breast for a couch and a covering for its young. And if man steals the nest, the mother still continues upon herself the cruel operation. When she has stripped off every feather, when there is nothing more to despoil but the flesh and the blood, the father takes his turn; so that the little one is clothed of themselves and their substance, by their devotion and their suffering. Montaigne, speaking of a cloak which had served his father, and which he loved to wear in remembrance of him, makes use of a tender phrase, which this poor nest recalls to my mind—" I wrapped myself up in my father."

THE WING.

THE WING.

Wings! wings! to sweep
O'er mountain high and valley deep
Wings! that my heart may rest
In the radiant morning's breast.

" Wings! to hover free
O'er the dawn-empurpled sea.
Wings! 'bove life to soar,
And beyond death for evermore."

RUCKERT.

IT is the cry of the whole earth, of the world, of all life; it is that which every species of animals or plants utters in a hundred diverse tongues—the voice which issues from the very rock and the inorganic creation: ' Wings! we seek for wings, and the power of flight and motion!"

Yea; the most inert bodies rush greedily into the chemical transformations which will make them part and parcel of the current of the universal life, and bestow upon them the organs of movement and fermentation.

Yea; the vegetables, fettered by their immovable roots, expand their secret loves towards a winged existence, and commend themselves to the winds, the waters, the insects, in quest of a life beyond their narrow limits—of that gift of flight which nature has refused to them.

We contemplate pityingly those rudimentary animals, the unau and the aï, sad and suffering images of man, which cannot advance a step without a groan—sloths or *tardigrades*. The names by which we identify them we might justly reserve for ourselves. If slowness be relative to the desire of movement, to the constantly futile effort to progress, to advance, to act, the true *tardigrade* is man. His faculty of dragging himself from one point of the earth to another, the ingenious instruments which he has recently invented in aid of that faculty—all this does not lessen his adhesion to the earth; he is not the less firmly chained to it by the tyranny of gravitation.

I see upon earth but one order of created beings which enjoy the power of ignoring or beguiling, by their freedom and swiftness of motion, this universal sadness of impotent aspiration; I mean those beings which belong to earth, so to speak, only by the tips of their wings;

which the air itself cradles and supports, most frequently without being otherwise connected with them than by guiding them at their need and their caprice.

A life of ease, yet sublime! With what a glance of scorn may the weakest bird regard the strongest, the swiftest of quadrupeds—a tiger, a lion! How it may smile to see them in their utter power-lessness bound, fastened to the earth, which they terrify with vain and useless roaring—with the nocturnal wailings that bear witness to the bondage of the so-called king of animals, fettered, as we are all, in that inferior existence which hunger and gravitation equally prepare for us!

Oh, the fatality of the appetites! the fatality of motion which compels us to drag our unwilling limbs along the earth! Implacable heaviness which binds each of our feet to the dull, rude element wherein death will hereafter resolve us, and says, "Son of the earth, to the earth thou belongest! A moment released from its bosom, thou shalt lie there henceforth for ages."

Do not let us inveigh against nature; it is assuredly the sign that we inhabit a world still in its first youth, still in a state of barbarism—a world of essay and apprenticeship in the grand series of the stars, one of the elementary stages of the sublime initiation. This planet is the world of a child. And thou, a child thou art. From this lower school thou shalt be emancipated also; thy wings shall be majestic and powerful. Thou shalt win and deserve, while here, by the sweat of thy brow, a step forward in liberty.

Let us make an experiment. Ask of the bird while still in the egg what he would wish to be; give him the option. Wilt thou be a man, and share in that royalty of the globe which men have won by art and toil?

No, he will immediately reply. Without calculating the immense exertion, the labour, the sweat, the care, the life of slavery by which we purchase sovereignty, he will have but one word to say: "A king myself, by birth, of space and light, why should I abdicate when man, in his loftiest ambition, in his highest aspirations after happiness and freedom, dreams of becoming a bird, and taking unto himself wings?"

It is in his sunniest time, his first and richest existence, in his day-dreams of youth, that man has sometimes the good fortune to forget that he *is* a man, a slave to hard fate, and chained to earth. Behold, yonder, him who flies abroad, who hovers, who dominates over the world, who swims in the sunbeam; he enjoys the ineffable felicity of embracing at a glance an infinity of things which yesterday he could see only one by one! Obscure enigma of detail, suddenly made luminous to him who perceives its unity! To see the world beneath one's self, to embrace, to love it! How divine, how lofty a dream! Do not wake me, I pray you, never wake me! But what is this? Here again are day, uproar, and labour; the harsh iron hammer, the ear-piercing bell with its voice of steel, dethrone and dash me headlong; my wings are rent. Dull earth, I fall to earth; bruised and bent, I return to the plough.

When, at the close of the last century, man formed the daring idea of giving himself up to the winds, of mounting in the air without rudder, or oar, or means of guidance, he proclaimed aloud that at length he had secured his pinions, had eluded nature, and conquered gravitation. Cruel and tragical catastrophes gave the lie to this ambition. He studied the economy of the bird's wing, he undertook to imitate it; rudely enough he counterfeited its inimitable mechanism. We saw with terror, from a column of a hundred feet high, a poor human bird, armed with huge wings, dart into air, wrestle with it, and dash headlong into atoms.

The gloomy and fatal machine, in its laborious complexity, was a sorry imitation of that admirable arm (far superior to the human one), that system of muscles, which co-operate among themselves in so vigorous and lively a movement. Disjointed and relaxed, the human wing lacked especially the all-powerful muscle which connects the shoulder with the chest (the *humerus* with the *sternum*), and communicates its impetus to the thunderous flight of the falcon. The instrument acts so directly on the mover, the oar on the rower, and

unites with him so perfectly, that the impetuous frigate-bird sweeps
along at the rate of eighty leagues an hour, five or six times swifter
than our most rapid railway trains, outstripping the hurricane, and
with no rival but the lightning.

But even if our poor imitators had exactly imitated the wing, nothing would have been accomplished.   They, then, had copied the *form*,
but not the *internal structure*.   They thought that the bird's power of
ascension lay in its flight alone, forgetting the secret auxiliary which
nature conceals in the plumage and the bones.   The mystery, the
true marvel lies in the faculty with which she endows the bird, of

rendering itself light or heavy at its will, of admitting more or less

of air into its specially constructed reservoirs. Would it grow light, it inflates its dimension, while diminishing its relative weight; by this means it spontaneously ascends in a medium heavier than itself. To descend or drop, it contracts itself, grows thin and small ; cutting through the air which supported and raised it in its former heavy condition. Here lay the great error, the cause of man's fatal ignorance. He assumed that the bird was a ship, not a balloon. He imitated the wing only; but the wing, however skilfully imitated, if not conjoined with this internal force, is but a certain means of destruction.

But this faculty, this rapid inhalation or expulsion of air, of swimming with a ballast variable at pleasure, whence does it proceed? From an unique, unheard-of power of respiration. The man who should inhale a similar quantity of air at one breath would be suffocated. The bird's elastic and powerful lung quaffs it, grows full of it, grows intoxicated with vigour and delight, and pours it abundantly into its bones, into its aerial cells. Each aspiration is renewed second after second with tremendous rapidity. The blood, ceaselessly vivified with fresh air, supplies each muscle with that inexhaustible energy which no other being possesses, and which belongs only to the elements.

The clumsy image of Antæus regaining strength each time he' touched the earth, his mother, does but rudely and weakly render an idea of this reality. The bird does not need to seek the air that he may be reinvigorated by touching it; the air seeks and flows into him—it incessantly kindles within him the burning fires of life.

It is this, and not the wing, which is so marvellous. Take the pinions of the condor, and follow in its track, when, from the summit of the Andes and their Siberian glaciers, it swoops down upon the glowing shore of Peru, traversing in a minute all the temperatures and all the climates of the globe, breathing at one breath the frightful mass of air—scorched, frozen, it matters not. You would reach the earth stricken as by thunder.

The smallest bird in this matter shames the strongest quadruped. Place me, says Toussenel, a chained lion in a balloon, and his harsh roaring will be lost in space. Far more powerful in voice and respiration, the little lark mounts upward, trilling its song, and makes itself heard when it can be seen no longer. Its light and joyous strain, uttered without fatigue, and costing nothing, seems the bliss of an invisible spirit which would fain console the earth.

Strength makes joy. The happiest of beings is the bird, because it feels itself strong beyond the limits of its action ; because, cradled and sustained by the breath of heaven, it floats and it rises without effort, like a dream. The boundless strength, the exalted faculty, obscure among inferior beings, but in the bird all clear and vital, of deriving at will its vigour from the maternal source, of drinking in life at full flood, is a divine intoxication.

The tendency of every human being—a tendency wholly rational, not arrogant, not impious—is to liken himself to Nature, the great Mother, to fashion himself after her image, to crave a share of the unwearied wings with which Eternal Love broods over the world.

Human tradition is fixed in this direction. Man does not wish to be a man, but an angel, a winged deity. The winged genii of Persia suggest the cherubim of Judea. Greece endows her Psyche with wings, and discovers the true name of the soul, ἄσθμα, *aspiration*. The soul has preserved her pinions; has passed at one flight through the shadowy Middle Age, and constantly increases in heavenly longings. More spotless and more glowing, she gives utterance to a prayer, breathed in the very depths of her nature and her prophetic ardour: " Oh, that I were a bird!" saith man.

Woman never doubts but that her offspring will become an angel. She has seen it so in her dreams.

Dreams or realities? Winged visions, raptures of the night, which we shall lament so bitterly in the morning! If ye really *were!* If, indeed, ye lived! If we had lost some of the causes of our regret! If, from stars to stars, re-united, and launched on an eternal flight, we all performed in companionship a happy pilgrimage through the illimitable goodness!

At times one is apt to believe it. Something whispers us that these dreams are not all dreams, but glimpses of a world of truth; momentary flashes revealed through the lower clouds; certain promises to be hereafter fulfilled, while the pretended reality it is that should be stigmatized as a foul delusion.

THE FIRST FLUTTERINGS OF THE WING.

THE FIRST FLUTTERINGS
OF THE WING.

THERE is never a man, unlettered, ignorant, exhausted, insensible, who can deny himself a sentiment of reverence, I might almost say of terror, on entering the halls of our Museum of Natural History.

No foreign collection, as far as my knowledge extends, produces this impression.

Others, undoubtedly, as the superb museum of Leyden, are richer in particular branches; but none are more complete, none more harmonious. This sublime harmony is felt instinctively; it imposes and seizes on the mind. The inattentive traveller, the chance visitor, is unwillingly affected; he pauses, and he dreams. In the presence of this vast enigma, of this immense hieroglyph which for the first time is displayed before him, he may consider himself fortunate if he can read a character or spell a letter.   How often have different classes of persons, surprised and tormented by such fantastic forms, inquired of us their meaning! A word has set them in the right path, a simple indication charmed them; they have gone away contented, and promising themselves to return. On the other hand, they who traversed this ocean of unknown objects without comprehending them, have departed fatigued and melancholy.

Let us express our wish that an administration so enlightened, and so high in the ranks of science, may return to the original constitution of the museum, which appointed *gardiens démonstrateurs*— attendants who were also cicerones—and will only admit as custodians of this treasure men who can understand it, and, on occasion, become its interpreters.

Another wish we dare to form is, that by the side of our renowned naturalists they will place those courageous navigators, those persevering travellers who, by their labours, their fruits, by a hundred times hazarding their lives, have procured for us these costly spoils.   Whatever their intrinsic value, it is, perhaps, increased by the heroism and grandeur of heart of these adventurers.   This charming colibris,* madam, a winged sapphire in which you could see only a useless object of personal decoration, do you know that an Azara† or a Lesson‡ has brought it from murderous forests where one breathes nothing but death?   This magnificent tiger, whose skin you admire, are you aware that before it could be planted here, there was a necessity that it should be sought after in the jungles, encountered face to face, fired at, struck in the forehead by the intrepid Levaillant?§   These illus-

* Family *Trochilidæ*.

† Felix de Azara was an eminent Spanish traveller, who died at Arragon in 1811.   He acted as one of the commissioners appointed to trace the boundary-line between the Spanish and Portuguese possessions in the New World.   His researches in Paraguay made many valuable contributions to natural history.—*Translator.*

‡ Lesson was a French traveller of repute; but his works are little known beyond the limits of his own country.—*Translator.*

§ François Levaillant was born at Paramaribo in Dutch Guiana, in 1753.   Passionately fond of natural history, and scarcely less fond of travel, he gratified both passions in 1780 by undertaking a series of explorations in Southern Africa.   His last journey extended a little beyond the tropic of Capricorn.   He returned to Europe in 1784, published several valuable works of travel and zoology, and died in 1824.—*Translator.*

trious travellers, ardent lovers of nature, often without means, often without assistance, have followed it into the deserts, watched and surprised it in its mysterious retreats, voluntarily enduring thirst and hunger and incredible fatigues; never complaining, thinking themselves too well recompensed, full of devotion, of gratitude at each fresh discovery; regretting nothing in such an event, not even the death of La Perouse* or Mungo Park, † death by shipwreck, or death among the savages.

Bid them live again here in our midst! If their lonely life flowed free from Europe for Europe's benefit, let their images be placed in the centre of the grateful crowd, with a brief exposition of their for-

* The unfortunate navigator, Jean François de Calaup, Comte de La Perouse, was born in 1741. At an early age he entered the French navy, rose to a high grade, and distinguished himself by his services against the English in North America. In 1783 he was appointed to command an expedition of discovery, and on the 1st of August 1785, sailed from Brest with two frigates, the *Boussole* and the *Astrolabe*. He reached Botany Bay in January 1788, and thenceforward was no more heard of for years. Several vessels were despatched to ascertain his fate, but could obtain no clue to it. In 1826, however, Captain Dillon, while sailing amongst the Queen Charlotte Islands, discovered at Wanicoro the remains of the shipwrecked vessels. A mausoleum and obelisk to the memory of their unfortunate commander were erected on the island in 1828.—*Translator*.

† Mungo Park, the illustrious African traveller (born near Selkirk in 1771), perished on his second expedition to the Niger towards the close of the year 1805. No exact information of his fate has been obtained, but from the evidence collected by Clapperton and Lander, it seems probable that he was drowned in attempting to navigate a narrow channel of the river in the territory of Houssa. Another account, however, represents him to have been murdered by the natives.—*Translator*.

tunate discoveries, their sufferings, and their sublime courage.   More
than one young man shall be moved by the sight of these heroes, and
depart to dream enthusiastically of following in their footsteps.

Herein lies the twofold grandeur of the place.   Its treasures were
sent by heroic men, and they were collected, classified, and harmonized
by illustrious physicists, to whom all things flowed as to a legitimate
centre, and whom their position, no less than their intellect, induced
to accomplish here the centralization of nature.

In the last century, the great movement of the sciences revolved
around a man of genius, influential by his rank, his social relations,
his fortune—M. the Count de Buffon.   All the donations of men of
science, travellers, and kings, came to him, and by him were classified
in this museum.   In our own days a grander spectacle has fixed upon
this spot the eager eyes of all the nations of the world, when two
mighty men (or rather two systems), Cuvier and Geoffroy, made
this their battle-field.   All the world enrolled itself on the one side
or the other; all took part in the strife, and despatched to the
Museum, either in support of or opposition to the experiments,
books, animals, or facts previously unknown.   Hence these collections,
which one might suppose to be dead, are really living; they still
throb with the recollections of the fray, are still animated by the lofty
minds which invoked all these beings to be the witnesses of their prolific struggle.

It is no fortuitous gathering yonder.   It consists of closely
connected series, formed and systematically arranged by profound
thinkers.   Those species which form the most curious transitions
between the genera are richly represented.   There you may see, far
more fully than elsewhere, what Linné and Lamarck have said, that
just as our museums gradually grew richer, became more complete,
exhibited fewer *lacunœ*, we should be constrained to acknowledge
that nature does nothing abruptly, in all things proceeds by gentle
and insensible transitions.   Wherever we seem to see in her works a
bound, a chasm, a sudden and inharmonious interval, let us ascribe
the fault to ourselves ; that blank is our own ignorance.

Let us pause for a few moments at the solemn passages where
life seems still to oscillate uncertain, and Nature appears to question
herself, to examine her own volition. " Shall I be fish or mammal?"
says the creature.   It falters, and remains a fish, but warm-
blooded; belongs to the mild race of lamantins and seals.   " Shall I
be bird or quadruped?"   A great question; a perplexed hesitancy—
a prolonged and changeful combat.   All its various phases are dis-
cussed; the diverse solutions of the problems naïvely suggested and
realized by fantastic beings like the ornithorhynchus, which has
nothing of the bird but the beak; like the poor bat, a tender and

innocent animal in its family-circle, but whose undefined form makes
it grim-looking and unfortunate.   You perceive that nature has

sought in it *the wing*, and found only a hideous membranous skin,
which nevertheless performs a wing's function :

" I am a bird ; see you my wings ? "

Yes ; but even the wing does not make the bird.

Place yourself towards the centre of the museum, and close to
the clock.   There you perceive, on your left, the first rudiment
of the wing in the penguin of the southern pole, and its brother,
the Arctic auk, one degree more developed ; scaly winglets, whose
glittering feathers rather recall the fish than the bird.   On land
the creature is feeble ; but while earth is difficult for it, air is
impossible.   Do not complain too warmly.   Its prescient mother

destines it for the Polar Seas, where it will need only to paddle.
She clothes it carefully in a fine coat of fat and an impenetrable
covering.   She will have it warm among the icebergs.   Which is the
better means ?   It seems as if she had hesitated, had wavered.   By
the side of the booby we see with surprise an essay at quite another

genus, yet one not less remarkable as a maternal precaution.   I refer
to a very rare gorfou—which I have seen in no other museum—
attired in the rough skin of a quadruped, resembling a goat's fleece,
but more glossy, perhaps, in the living animal, and certainly impermeable to water.

To unite together the birds which do not fly, we must find the
connecting-link in the navigator of the desert—the bird-camel, the
ostrich, resembling the camel itself in its internal structure.   At least,
if its imperfect wings cannot raise it above the earth, they assist it
powerfully in walking, and endow it with extraordinary swiftness:
it is the sail with which it skims its arid African ocean.

Let us return to the penguin, the true starting-point of the
series—to the penguin, whose rudimentary pinion cannot be employed
as a sail, does not aid it in walking, is only an indication, like an
after-thought of nature.

She loosens her bonds, and rises with difficulty in her first attempt
at flight by means of two strange figures, which appear to us both
grotesque and pretentious.   The penguin is not of these; a simple,
silly creature, you see that it never had the ambition to fly.   But
here are they who emancipate themselves, who seem in quest of the
adornment or the grace of motion.   The gorfou may be taken for a

penguin which has decided to quit its condition.   It assumes a
coquettish tuft of plumes, that throws into high relief its ugliness.

The shapeless puffin, which seems the very caricature of a caricature, the paroquet, resembles it in its great beak, rudely chipped, but without edge or strength.   Tail-less and ill-balanced, it may always be upset by the weight of its large head.   It ventures, nevertheless, to flutter about, at the hazard of toppling over.   It swoops nobly close to the surface of earth, and is, perhaps, the envy of the penguins and the seals.   Sometimes it even risks itself at sea—ill-fated ship, which the lightest breeze will wreck !

It is, however, impossible to deny that the first flight is taken. Birds of various kinds carry on the enterprise more successfully.   The rich genus of *divers* (Brachypteræ), in its species widely different, connects the sailor-birds with the natatores, or swimmers: those, with wings perfected, with a bold and secure flight, accomplish the longest voyages ; these, still clothed with the glittering feathers of the penguin, frisk and sport at the bottom of the seas.   They want but fins and respiratory organs to become actual fishes.   They are alternately masters of both elements, air and water.

TRIUMPH OF THE WING.

TRIUMPH OF THE WING.

THE FRIGATE BIRD.

LET us not attempt to particularize all the intermediate gradations. Let us proceed to yonder snow-white bird, which I perceive floating on high among the clouds; the bird conspicuous everywhere —on water, on land; on rocks alternately concealed and exposed by the waves; the bird which one loves to watch, familiar as it is, and greedy, and which might well be named " the little vulture of the seas." I refer to those myriads of petrels, or gulls, with whose hoarse cries every waste resounds. Find me, if you can, creatures endowed with fuller liberty. Day and night, south or north, sea or shore, dead prey or living, all is one to them. Using everything, at home everywhere, they indifferently display their white sails from the waves to the heaven; the fresh breeze, ever shifting and changing, is a bounteous wind always blowing in the direction they most desire.

What are they but air, sea, the elements, which have taken wing
and fly? I know nothing of it. To see their gray eye, stern and
cold (never successfully imitated in our museums), is to see the gray,
indifferent sea of the north in all its icy impassiveness. What do I
say? That sea exhibits more emotion. At times phosphorescent
and electrical, it will rise into strong animation. Old Father Ocean,
saturnine and passionate, often revolves, under his pale countenance,
a host of thoughts. His sons, the sea-gulls, have less of animal life

than he has. They fly, with their dead eyes seeking some dead prey;
and in congregated flocks they expedite the destruction of the great
carcasses which float upon the sea for their behoof. Not ferocious in
aspect, amusing the voyager by their sports, and by frequent glimpses
of their snowy pinions, they speak to him of remote lands, of the shores
which he leaves behind or is about to visit, of absent or hoped-for
friends. And they are useful to him, also, by announcing and pre-
dicting the coming storm. Ofttimes their sail expanded warns him
to furl his own.

For do not suppose that when the tempest breaks they deign to
fold their wings. Far from this: it is then that they set forth. The
storm is their harvest time; the more terrible the sea, so much the
less easily can the fish escape from these daring fishers. In the Bay
of Biscay, where the ocean-swell, driven from the north-west, after

traversing the Atlantic, arrives in mighty billows, swollen to enormous heights, with a terrific clash and shock, the tranquil petrels labour imperturbably. "I saw them," says M. de Quatrefages, "describe in the air a thousand curves, plunge between two waves, reappear with a fish. Swiftest when they followed the wind, slowest when they confronted it, they nevertheless poised always with the same ease, and never appeared to give a stroke of the wing the more than in the calmest weather. And yet the billows mounted up the slopes, like cataracts reversed, as high as the platform of Nôtre Dame, and their spray higher than Montmartre. They did not appear more moved by it."

Man has not their philosophy. The seaman is powerfully affected when, at the decline of day, a sudden night darkening over the sea, he descries, hovering about his barque, an ominous little pigeon, a bird of funereal black. *Black* is not the fitting word ; black would be less gloomy : the true tint is that of a smoky-brown, which cannot be defined. It is a shadow of hell, an evil vision, which strides along the waters, breasts the billows, crushes under its feet the tempest. The stormy petrel (or "St. Peter") is the horror of the seaman, who sees in it, according to his belief, a living curse. Whence does it come? How is it able to rise at such enormous distances from all land? What wills it? What does it come in quest of, if not of a wreck? It sweeps to and fro impatiently, and already selects the corpses which its accomplice, the atrocious and iniquitous sea, will soon deliver up to its mercies.

Such are the fables of fear. Less panic-stricken minds would see in the poor bird another ship in distress, an imprudent navigator, which has also been surprised far from shore and without an asylum. Our vessel is for him an island, where he would fain repose. The track of the barque, which rides through both wind and wave, is in itself a refuge, a succour against fatigue. Incessantly, with nimble flight, he places the rampart of the vessel between himself and the tempest. Timid and short-sighted, you see it only when it brings the night. Like ourselves, it dreads the storm—it trembles with fear—it would fain escape—and like you, O seaman, it sighs, "What will become of my little ones?"

But the black hour passes, day reappears, and I see a small blue point in the heaven. Happy and serene region, which has rested in peace far above the hurricane! In that blue point, and at an elevation of ten thousand feet, royally floats a little bird with enormous pens. A gull? No; its wings are black. An eagle? No; the bird is too small.

It is the little ocean-eagle, first and chief of the winged race, the daring navigator who never furls his sails, the lord of the tempest, the scorner of all peril—the man-of-war or frigate-bird.

We have reached the culminating point of the series commenced by the wingless bird. Here we have a bird which is virtually nothing more than wings: scarcely any body—barely as large as that of the domestic cock—while his prodigious pinions are fifteen feet in span. The great problem of flight is solved and overpassed, for the power of flight seems useless. Such a bird, naturally sustained by such supports, need but allow himself to be borne along. The storm bursts; he mounts to lofty heights, where he finds tranquillity. The poetic metaphor, untrue when applied to any other bird, is no exaggeration when applied to him : literally, he sleeps upon the storm.

When he chooses to oar his way seriously, all distance vanishes : he breakfasts at the Senegal ; he dines in America.

Or, if he thinks fit to take more time, and amuse himself *en route*, he can do so. He may continue his progress through the night indefinitely, certain of reposing himself. Upon what ? On his huge motionless pinion, which takes upon itself all the weariness of the voyage ; or on the wind, his slave, which eagerly hastens to cradle him.

Observe, moreover, that this strange being is gifted with the proud prerogative of fearing nothing in this world. Little, but strong and intrepid, he braves all the tyrants of the air. He can despise, if need be, the pygargue and the condor : those huge unwieldy creatures will with great difficulty have put themselves in motion when he shall have already achieved a distance of ten leagues.

Oh, it is then that envy seizes us, when, amid the glowing azure of the Tropics, at incredible altitudes, almost imperceptible in the dim remoteness, we see him triumphantly sweeping past us—this black, solitary bird, alone in the waste of heaven : or, at the most, at a lower elevation, the snow-white sea-swallow crosses his flights in easy grace !

Why dost not thou take me upon thy pens, O king of the air, thou fearless and unwearied master of space, whose wondrously swift flight annihilates time ? Who so elevated as thou art above the mean fatalities of existence ?

One thing, however, has astonished me: that, when contemplated from near at hand, the first of the winged kingdom should have nothing of that serenity which a free life promises. His eye is cruelly hard, severe, mobile, unquiet. His vexed attitude is that of some unhappy sentinel doomed, under pain of death, to keep watch over the infinity of ocean. He visibly exerts himself to see afar. And if his vision does not avail him, the doom is on his dark countenance; nature condemns him, he dies.

On looking at him closely, you perceive that he has no feet. Or at all events, his feet being palmate and exceedingly short, can neither walk nor perch. With a formidable beak, he has not the talons of a true eagle of the sea. A pseudo-eagle, and superior to the true in his daring as in his powers of flight, he is deficient, however, in strength and invincible grasp. He strikes and slays : can he seize?

Thence arises his life of uncertainty and hazard—the life of a corsair and a pirate rather than of a mariner—and the fixed inquiry

ever legible on his countenance: "Shall I feed? Shall I have wherewithal to nourish my little ones this evening?"

The immense and superb apparatus of his wings becomes on land

a danger and an embarrassment.   To raise himself he needs a strong
wind and a lofty station, a promontory, a rock.   Surprised on a
sandy level, on the banks, the low reefs where he sometimes halts,
the frigate-bird is defenceless; in vain he threatens, he strikes, for a
blow from a stick will overcome him.

At sea, those vast wings, of such admirable utility in ascent, are
ill-fitted for skimming the surface of the water.   When wetted, they
may over-weight and sink him.   And thereupon, woe to the bird !
He belongs to the fishes, he nourishes the mean tribes on which he
had relied for his own behoof; the game eats the hunter, the ensnarer
is ensnared.

And yet, what shall he do ?   His food lies in the waters.   He is
ever compelled to draw near them, to return to them, to skim incessantly the hateful and prolific sea which threatens to engulf him.

Thus, then, this being so well-armed, winged, superior to all
others in power of flight and vision as in daring, leads but a trembling and precarious life.   He would die of hunger had he not the
ingenuity to create for himself a purveyor, whom he cheats of his food.
His ignoble resource, alas, is to attack a dull and timorous bird, the
noddy, famous as a fisher.   The frigate-bird, which is of no larger
dimensions, pursues him, strikes him on the neck with his beak, and
constrains him to yield up his prey.   All these incidents transpire in
the air; before the fish can fall, he catches it on its passage.

If this resource fail, he does not shrink from attacking man.
" On landing at Ascension Island," says a traveller, " we were assailed
by some frigate-birds.   One tried to snatch a fish out of my very
hand.   Others alighted on the copper where the meat was being
cooked to carry it off, without taking any notice of the sailors who
were around it."

Dampier saw some of these birds, sick, aged, or crippled, perched
upon the rocks which seemed their sanatorium, levying contributions
upon the young noddies, their vassals, and nourishing themselves on
the results of their fishery.   But in the vigour of their prime they do
not rest on earth; living like the clouds, constantly floating on their

vast wings from one world to the other, patiently awaiting their fortune, and piercing the infinite heaven—the infinite waters—with implacable glance.

The lord of the winged race is he who does not rest. The chief of navigators is he who never reaches his bourne. Earth and sea are almost equally prohibited to him. He is for ever banished.

Let us envy nothing. No existence is really free here below, no career is sufficiently extensive for us, no power of flight sufficiently great, no wing can satisfy. The most powerful is but a temporary substitute. The soul waits, demands, and hopes for others :—

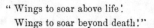

" Wings to soar above life!
Wings to soar beyond death!"

[NOTE.—*The Frigate-Bird.* This interesting bird (*Tachypetes*) is allied to the cormorants, but differs from them in the possession of a forked tail, short feet, a curved beak, and extraordinary spread of wing. Its plumage is coloured of a rich purple black, but the beak is varied with vermilion red, and the throat with patches of white. It is an inhabitant of the Tropics, where it lives a predatory life, forcing the gannet and the gull to disgorge their prey, and retiring to breed in lonely uninhabited islands.

Of its voracity, Dr. Chamberlaine gives a curious illustration. When the fishermen are pursuing their vocation on the sand-banks in Kingston Harbour, Jamaica, the gulls, pelicans, and other sea-birds gather round in swarms, and as the loaded net is hauled ashore, pounce upon their struggling prey. But no sooner does this take place, than the frigate-birds attack them with such furious violence that they are glad to surrender their hard-earned booty to antagonists so formidable.

The lightness of his body, his short tarsi, his enormous spread of wing, together with his long, slender, and forked tail, all combine to give this bird a superiority over his tribe, not only in length and swiftness of flight, but also in the capability of maintaining himself on extended pinions in his aerial realm, where, at times, he will soar so high that his figure can scarce be discerned by the spectator in this nether world.—*Translator.*]

THE SHORES.

THE SHORES.

DECAY OF CERTAIN SPECIES.

I HAVE frequently observed, in my days of sadness, a being sadder than myself, which Melancholy might have chosen for its symbol: I mean the Dreamer of the Marshes, the meditative bird that, in all seasons, standing solitarily before the dull waters, seems, along with his image, to plunge in their mirror his monotonous thought.

His noble ebon-black crest, his pearl-gray mantle—this semi-regal mourning contrasts with his puny body and transparent leanness. When flying, the poor heron displays but a couple of wings; low as is the elevation to which he rises, there is no longer any question of his body—he becomes invisible. An animal truly aerial, to bear so light a frame,

the heron has enough, nay, he has a foot too many; he folds under his
wing the other; and nearly always his lame figure is thus defined
against the sky in a fantastical hieroglyph.

Whoever has lived in history, in the study of fallen races and
empires, is tempted to see herein
an image of decay.   Yonder bird
is a great ruined lord, a dethroned king, or I am much mistaken.   No creature issues from
Nature's hands in so miserable a
condition.   Therefore I ventured
to interrogate this dreamer, and I
said to him from a distance the
following words, which his most
delicate hearing caught exactly:—
" My fisher-friend, wouldst thou
oblige me by explaining (without
abandoning thy present position),
why, always so melancholy, thou
seemest doubly melancholy to-day?
Hath thy prey failed thee?   Have
the too subtle fish deceived thine
eyes?   Does the mocking frog defy
thee from the bottom of the
waters?"

" No; neither fish nor frogs
have made sport of the heron.   But
the heron laughs at himself, despises
himself, when he remembers the
glory of his noble race, and the bird of the olden times.

"Thou wouldst know wherefore I dream?   Ask the Indian chief
of the Cherokees, or the Iowas, why for long days he leans his head
upon his hand, marking on the tree before him an object which was
never there?

" The earth was our empire, the realm of the aquatic birds in the Transitional age when, young and fresh, she emerged from the waters. An era of strife, of battle, but of abundant subsistence. Not a heron then but earned his life. There was need neither to attack nor pursue; the prey hunted the hunter; it whistled, or it croaked on every side. Millions of creatures of undefined natures, bird-frogs, winged fish, infested the uncertain limits of the two elements. What would ye have done, ye feeble mortals, the latest-born of the world? The Bird made ready your earth. Colossal encounters were waged against the enormous monster-births of the ooze; the son of air, the bird, attaining the dimensions of an Anak, shrunk not from battle with the giant. If your ungrateful histories have not traced these events, God's grand record narrates them in the depths of the earth, where she deposits the conquered and the conquerors, the monsters exterminated by us, and we who have exterminated them.

" Your lying myths make us contemporaries of a human Hercules. What had his club availed against the plesiosaurus? Who would have met, face to face, the horrible leviathan? The capacity of flight was absolutely needed, the strong intrepid wing which from the loftiest height bore downwards the Herculean bird, the epiornis, an eagle twenty feet in stature, and fifty feet from wing-tip to wing-tip, the implacable hunter, who, lord of three elements, in the air, in the water, and in the deep slime, pursued the dragon with ceaseless hostility.

" Man had perished a hundred times. Through our agency man became possible on a pacified earth. But who will be astonished that these awful wars, which lasted for myriads of years, spent the conquerors, wearied the winged Hercules, transformed him into a feeble Perseus, a pale and lustreless memory of our heroic times ?

" Lowered in strength and stature, but not in heart, famished by our very victory, by the disappearance of evil races, by the division of the elements which held our prey concealed at the bottom of the waters, we in our turn were hunted upon the earth, in the forests and the marsh, by those new-comers who, without our help, had never been. The malice and dexterity of the woodman were fatal to our nests. Like a coward, in the thick of the branches which impede flight and shackle combat, he laid his hand on our young ones. A new war, and a less fortunate one, this, which Homer calls the War of the Pigmies and the Cranes. The lofty intelligence of the cranes, their truly military tactics, have not prevented man their enemy from gaining the advantage by a thousand execrable arts. Time was on his side, and earth, and nature: she moves forward, drying up the earth, exhausting the marshes, narrowing the undefined region where we reigned. It will be with us, in the end, as with the beaver. Many species perish: another century, perhaps, and the heron *will have* lived."

The story is too true. Except those species which have taken their side, have abandoned earth, have given themselves up frankly and unreservedly to the liquid element; except the divers, the cormorant, the wise pelican, and a few others, the aquatic tribes seem in a state of decay. Restlessness and sobriety maintain them still. It is this persistent anxiety which has gifted the pelican with a peculiar organ, hollowing for her under her distended beak a movable reservoir, a living sign of economy and of attentive foresight.

Others, skilful voyagers, like the swan, live by constantly changing their abode. But the swan herself, which, though uneatable, is trained by man on account of her beauty and her grace— the swan, formerly so common in Italy, and to which Virgil so constantly refers, is now very rare there. In vain the traveller would seek for those snow-white flotillas which covered with their sails the waters of the Mincio, the marshes of Mantua; which mourned for Phaëton in despite of his sisters, or in their sublime flight, pursuing the stars with harmonious song, repeated to them the name of Varus.*

That song, of which all antiquity speaks, is it a fable? These organs of singing, which are so largely developed in the swan, were

* See Virgil, "Georgics."

they always useless? Did they never disport themselves in happy freedom when enjoying a more genial atmosphere, and spending the greater portion of the year in the mild climates of Greece and Italy? One might be tempted to believe it. The swan, driven back to the north, where his amours secure mystery and repose, has sacrificed his song, has gained the accent of barbarism, or become voiceless. The muse is dead; the bird has survived.

Gregarious, disciplined, full of tactic and resources, the crane, the superior type of intelligence among these species, might contrive, one would fancy, to prosper, and to maintain herself everywhere in her ancient royalty. She has lost two kingdoms, however: France, where she now appears only as a bird of passage; England, where she rarely ventures to deposit her eggs.

The heron, in the days of Aristotle, was full of industry and sagacity The ancients consulted him in reference to fine weather or tempest, as one of the gravest of augurs. Fallen in the mediæval days, but preserving his beauty, his heavenward flight, he was still a prince, a feudal bird ; kings esteemed it kingly sport to hunt him, and considered him a meet quarry for the

noble falcon.   And so keenly was he hunted, that already, in the reign of Francis I., he had grown rare : that monarch lodged him near his own palace at Fontainebleau, and established there some heronries. Two or three centuries pass, and Buffon can still believe that there are no provinces in France where heronries could not be found.   In our own days, Toussenel knows of but one in all the country—at least in its northern districts, in Champagne : a wood between Rheims and Epernay conceals the last asylum where the poor lonely bird still dares to hide his loves.

Lonely !   In that lies his condemnation.   Less gregarious than the crane, less domesticated than the stork, he seems to have grown harsh towards his progeny, towards the mate whom he loves.   His brief rare fits of desire scarcely beguile him for a day from his melancholy. He cares little for life.   In captivity he often refuses nourishment, and pines away without complaint and without regret.

The aquatic birds, creatures of great experience, for the most part reflective and learned in two elements, were, at their palmiest epoch, more advanced than many others. They well deserved the care of man. All of them possessed merits of diverse originality. The social instinct of the cranes, and their various imitative talent, rendered them amusing and agreeable. The joviality of the pelican, and his joyous humour; the tenderness of the goose, and his strong faculty of attachment; and, finally, the good disposition of the storks, their piety towards their aged parents, confirmed by so many witnesses, formed between this world and our own firm ties of sympathy, which human levity ought not barbarously to have rent asunder.

[NOTE.—*Heronries in England.* The heron, though rare in England, is certainly not so scarce as he seems to be in France, perhaps because it is against the laws of sport to hunt him. In some districts the man who shot a heron would be regarded with as much scorn as if he had killed a fox. He is a very rapacious bird, and it is asserted that, on an average, he will destroy daily half a hundred small roach and dace.

There is a fine heronry at Cobham, near Gravesend, in Kent, the seat of the Earl of Darnley. Another, in Great Sowdens Wood, on the Rye road, one mile from Udimere, in Sussex, contains fully four hundred nests. That at Parham, the Hon. R. Curzon's beautiful seat has quite a history.

The original birds were brought from Wales to Penshurst, by the Earl of Leicester's steward, in the reign of James I. Thence, some two centuries later, they migrated to Michel Grove, at Angmering. It may be about twenty years since that the Duke of Norfolk caused two or three trees to be felled near their retreat, and the offended birds immediately commenced their migrations, and, in the course of three seasons, all assembled in Parham Woods. Here, in the thick shelter of pine and spruce-fir, are now about fifty-seven nests. (See Knox's " Ornithological Rambles in Kent and Sussex.")—*Translator*.]

THE HERONRIES OF AMERICA.

THE HERONRIES OF AMERICA.

WILSON, THE ORNITHOLOGIST.

THE decay of the heron is less perceptible in America. He is not so frequently hunted. The solitudes are of vaster dimensions. He can still find, among his beloved marshes, gloomy and almost impenetrable forests. In these shadowy recesses he is more gregarious : ten or fifteen "domestic exiles" establish themselves in the same locality, or at but a short distance from each other. The complete obscurity which the huge cedars throw over the livid waters re-assures and rejoices them. Towards the summit of these trees they build with sticks a wide platform, which they cover with small branches : this is the residence of the family, and the shelter of their loves; there, the eggs are laid and hatched in quiet, the young are taught to fly, and all those paternal lessons are given which will perfect the young fisher. They have little cause to fear the intrusion of man into their peaceful retreats : these they find near the sea-shore, especially in North and South Carolina, in low swampy levels, the haunt of yellow fever. Such morasses—an ancient arm of the sea or a river, an old swamp left behind in the gradual recession of the waters—extend sometimes over a length of five or six miles, and a breadth of one mile.   The entry is not very inviting : a barrier of trees confronts you, their trunks perfectly upright and stripped of branches, fifty or sixty feet high, and bare to the very summit, where they mingle and bring together their leafy arches of sombre green, so as to shed upon the waters an ominous twilight.   What waters !   A seething mass of leaves and débris, where the old stems rise pell-mell one upon another ; the whole of a muddy yellow colour, coated on the surface with a green frothy moss.   Advance, and the seemingly firm expanse is a quicksand, into which you plunge.   A laurel-tree at each step intercepts you ; you cannot pass without a painful struggle with their branches, with wrecks of trees, with laurels constantly springing up afresh.   Rare gleams of light shoot athwart the darkness, and the silence of death prevails in these terrible regions.   Except the melancholy notes of two or three small birds, which you catch at intervals, or the hoarse cry of the heron, all is dumb and desolate ; but when the wind rises, from the summit of the trees comes the heron's moans and sighs.   If the storm bursts, these great naked cedars, these tall "ammiral's masts," waver and clash together ; the forest roars, cries, groans, and imitates with singular exactness the voices of wolves, and bears, and all the beasts of prey.

It was not then without astonishment that, about 1805, the heron, thus securely settled, saw a rare face, a man's, roaming under their cedars, and in the open swamp.   One man alone was capable of visiting them in their haunts, a patient indefatigable traveller, no less courageous than peaceable—the friend and the admirer of birds, Alexander Wilson.

If these people had been acquainted with their visitor's character, far from feeling terrified at his appearance, they would undoubtedly have gone forth to meet him, and, with clapping of wings and loud cries, have given him an amicable salute, a fraternal ovation.

In those terrible years when man waged against man the most destructive war that had ever been known, there lived in Scotland a man of peace. A poor Paisley weaver,* in his damp dull lodging, he dreamed of nature, of the infinite liberty of the woods, and, above all, of the wingèd life. Crippled in means, and doomed by want, his very bondage inspired him with an ecstatic love of light and flight. If he did not take to himself wings, it was because that sublime gift is, upon earth, only the dream and hope of another world.

* Alexander Wilson, the eminent ornithologist, was born at Paisley in 1766. He was bred a weaver, but emigrating to the United States in 1794, found means to pursue the studies for which he had a natural bias, and in which he earned an enduring reputation. The first volume of his "American Ornithology" was published in 1808. He died of dysentery, in August 1813.—*Translator.*

At first he attempted to gratify his love of birds by the purchase of those illustrated works which pretend to represent them. Clumsy caricatures, which convey but a ridiculous idea of their form, and none at all of their movement; and what *is* the bird deprived of grace and motion? These did not suffice. He took a decisive resolution : to abandon everything, his trade, his country. A new Robinson Crusoe, he was willing, by a voluntary ship-wreck, to exile himself to the solitudes of America ; where he might see with his own eyes, observe, describe, and paint. He then remembered one little fact : that he was wholly unable to draw, to paint, or to write. But this strong and patient man, whom no difficulties could discourage, soon learned to write, and to write an excellent style. A good writer, a minutely accurate artist, with a delicate and certain hand, he seemed, under the guid-ance of Nature, his mother and mistress, less to learn than to remember.

Provided with these weapons, he plunges into the desert, the forest, and the pestiferous savannahs ; becomes the friends of buffaloes and the guest of bears ; lives upon wild fruits, under the splendid ceiling of heaven. Wherever he chances to observe a rare bird, he halts, encamps, and is " at home." What, indeed, is there to hurry him onward? He has no house to recall him, and neither wife nor child awaits him. He has a family, it is true : that great family which he observes and describes. And friends, he has *them* too : those which have not yet learned to mistrust man, and which perch upon his tree, and chatter with him.

And, O birds, you are right ; you have there a truly loyal friend, who will secure you many others, who will teach men to understand you, being himself as a bird in thought and heart. One day, perhaps, the traveller, penetrating into your solitudes, and seeing some of you fluttering and sparkling in the sun, will be tempted with the hope of spoil, but will bethink himself of Wilson. Why kill the friends of Wilson? And when this name flashes on his memory, he will lower his gun.

I do not see, let me add, why we should extend to infinity our massacre of birds, or, at least, of these species which are represented in our museums, or in the museums painted by Wilson, and his disciple Audubon, whose truly royal book, exhibiting both the race, and the egg, the nest, the forest, and the landscape, almost rivals nature.

These great observers have one speciality which separates them from all others. Their feeling is so delicate, so precise, that no generalities could satisfy it; they must always examine the individual. God, I think, knows nothing of our classifications : he created such and such a creature, and gives but little heed to the imaginary lines with which we isolate the species. In the same manner, Wilson knew nothing of birds in the mass; but such an individual, of such an age, with such plumage, in such circumstances. He knows it, has seen it, has seen it again and again, and he will tell you what it does, what it eats, how it comports itself, and will relate certain adventures, certain anecdotes of its life. "I knew a woodpecker. I have frequently seen a Baltimore." When he uses these expressions, you may wholly trust yourself to him ; they mean that he has held close relations with them in a species of friendly and family intimacy. Would that we knew the men with whom we transact business as well as Wilson knew the bird *qua*, or the heron of the Carolinas !

It is easily understood, and not difficult to imagine, that when this *bird-man* returned among men, he met with none that could comprehend him. His peculiarly novel originality, his marvellous exactness, his unique faculty of *individualization* (the only means of re-making of re-creating the living being), were the chief obstacles to his success. Neither publishers nor public cared for more than noble, lofty, and vague generalities, in faithful observance of Buffon's precept : To generalize is to ennoble ; therefore, adopt the word " general."

It required time, and, more than all, it required that this fertile genius should after his death inspire a similar genius, the accurate and patient Audubon, whose colossal work has astonished and subjugated the public, by demonstrating that the true and living in representation of individuality is nobler and more majestic than the forced products of the generalizing art.

Wilson's sweetness of disposition, so unworthily misunderstood, shines forth in his beautiful preface. To some it may appear infantine, but no innocent heart can be otherwise than moved by it.

" On a visit to a friend, I found that his young son, about eight or nine years of age, who had been brought up in the town, but was then living in the country, had just collected, while wandering in the fields, a fine nosegay of wild-flowers of every hue. He presented it to his mother, with the greatest animation, saying : ' Dear mamma, see what beautiful flowers I have gathered ! Oh, I could pluck a host of others which grow in our woods, and are still more lovely ! Shall I not bring you some more, mamma ?' She took the nosegay with a smile of tenderness, silently admired the simple and touching beauty of nature, and said to him, ' Yes, my son.' The child started off on the wings of happiness.

" I saw myself in that child, and was struck with the resemblance.

If my native country receive with gracious indulgence the specimens which I now humbly offer it, if it express a desire that *I should bring it some more*, my highest ambition will be satisfied.   For, as my little friend said, our woods are full of them ; I can gather numerous others which are still more beautiful."—(Philadelphia, 1808.)

THE COMBAT.

THE COMBAT.

THE TROPICAL REGIONS.

A LADY of our family, who resided in Louisiana, was nursing her young child. Every night her sleep was troubled by the strange sensation of a cold gliding object which sought to draw the milk from her breast. On one occasion she felt the same impression, and it aroused her. She sprang up, summoned her attendants; a light was brought; they searched every corner, turned over the bed, and at last discovered the frightful nursling—a serpent of great size and of a dangerous species. The horror which she felt instantly dried up her milk.

Levaillant relates that at the Cape of Good Hope, in a circle of friends, and during a quiet conversation, the lady of the house turned pale, and uttered a terrible cry. A serpent had crept up her legs, one of those whose sting is death in a couple of minutes. With great difficulty it was killed.

In India, a French soldier, resuming his knapsack which he had placed on the ground, discovered behind it the dangerous black serpent, the most venomous of his tribe. He was about to cut it in two when a merciful Hindu interposed, obtained its pardon, and took up the serpent. Stung by it, he died immediately.

Such are the terrors of nature in those formidable climates. But reptiles, now-a-days rare, are not the greatest curse. In all places and at all times it is now the insect. Insects everywhere, and in everything; they possess an infinity of means for attacking you; they walk, swim, glide, fly; they are in the air, and you breathe them. Invisible, they make known their presence by the most painful wounds. Recently, in one of our sea-ports, an official of the customs opened a parcel of papers brought from the colonies a long time previously. A fly furiously darted out of it; it pursued, it stung him; two days afterwards he was a corpse.

The hardiest of men, the buccaneers and filibusters, declared that of all dangers and of all pains they dreaded most the wounds of insects.

Frequently intangible, invisible, irresistible, they are destruction itself under an unavoidable form. How shall you oppose them when they make war upon you in legions? Once, at Barbadoes, the inhabitants observed an immense army of great ants, which, impelled by unknown causes, advanced in a serried column and in the same direction against the houses. To kill them was only trouble lost. There were no means of arresting their progress. At last an ingenious mind fortunately suggested that trains of gunpowder should be laid across their route, and set on fire. These volcanoes terrified them, and the torrent of invasion gradually turned aside.

No mediæval armoury, with all the strange weapons then made use of; no chirurgical implement factory, with the thousands of dreadful instruments invented by modern art, can be compared with the monstrous armour of Tropical insects—their pincers, their nippers, their teeth, their saws, their horns, their augers, all their tools of combat, of death, and of dissection, with which they come armed to the battle, with which they labour, pierce, cut, rend, and finely partition, with skill and dexterity equal to their furious blood-thirstiness.

Our grandest works may not defy the energetic force of these terrible legions. Give them a ship of the line—what do I say ? a town—to devour, and they charge at it with eager joy. In course of time they have excavated under Valentia, near Caraccas, vast abysses and catacombs ; the city is now literally suspended. A few individuals of this voracious tribe, unfortunately transported to Rochelle, have set to work to eat up the place, and already more than one edifice trembles upon timbers which are only externally sound, and at the core are rotten.

What would be the fate of a man abandoned to these insects ? One dares not think of it. An unfortunate wretch, while intoxicated, fell down near a carcass. The insects which were devouring the dead could not distinguish from it the living ; they took possession of his body, entered at every avenue, filled all the natural cavities. It was impossible to save him. He expired in the midst of frightful convulsions.

In those lands of fire, where the rapidity of decomposition renders every corpse dangerous, where all death threatens life, these terrible accelerators of the disappearance of animal bodies multiply *ad infinitum.* A corpse scarcely touches the earth before it is seized, attacked, disorganized, dissected. Only the bones are left. Nature, endangered by her own fecundity, invites, stimulates, encourages them by the heat, by the irritation of a world of spices and acrid substances. She makes them furious hunters, insatiable gluttons. The tiger and the lion, compared with the vulture, are mild, sober, moderate creatures ; but what is the vulture in the presence of an insect which, in four-and-twenty hours, consumes thrice its own weight ?

Greece personified nature under the calm and noble image of Cybele chariot-drawn by lions. India dreams of her god Siva, the divinity of life and death, who incessantly winks his eye, never gazing fixedly, because his single glance would reduce all the worlds to dust. How weak these fancies of men in the presence of the reality ! What avail their fictions before the burning centre where, by atoms or by seconds, life dies, is born, blazes, scintillates ?

Who could sustain the thunderous flash without reeling and without terror ?

Just, indeed, and legitimate, is the traveller's hesitancy at the entrance of these fearful forests where Tropical Nature, under forms oftentimes of great beauty, wages her keenest strife. It is the place to pause when one knows that the most formidable defence of the Spanish fortresses is found in a simple grove of cactus, which, planted around them, speedily swarms with serpents. You frequently detect there a strong odour of musk, a nauseous, a sinister odour. It tells you that you are treading on the very dust of the dead : the wreck of animals which possessed that peculiar savour, tiger-cats, and crocodiles, vultures, vipers, and rattle-snakes.

The peril is greatest, perhaps, in those virgin-forests where everything is eloquent of life, where nature's seething crucible eternally boils and bubbles.

Here and there their living shadows thicken with a threefold canopy—the colossal trees, the entwining and interlacing lianas, and herbs of thirty feet high with magnificent leaves. At intervals, these herbs sink into the ancient primeval slime ; while, at the height of a hundred feet, the lofty and puissant flowers break through the deep night to display themselves in the burning sun.

In the clearances—the narrow alleys where his rays penetrate— prevails a scintillation, an eternal murmuring, of beetles, butterflies, humming-birds, and fly-catchers—gems animated and mobile, which incessantly flutter to and fro. At night—a far more astonishing scene !—begins the fairylike illumination of shining fire-flies, which, by thousands of millions, weave fantastic arabesques and dazzling pageantries of light, magical scrolls of fire !

With all this splendour there lurks in the lower levels an obscure race, a hideous and foul world of caymans and water-serpents ! To the trunks of enormous trees the fanciful orchids, the well-loved daughters of fever, the children of a miasmatic atmosphere, quaint vegetable butterflies, suspend themselves in seeming motion. In these murderous solitudes they take their delight, and bathe in the putrid swamps, drink of the death which inspires them with vitality, and, by the caprice of their unheard-of colours, make sport of the intoxication of nature.

Do not yield—defend yourself—let not the fatal charm bow down your sinking head. Awake ! arouse ! under a hundred forms the danger surrounds you. Yellow fever lurks beneath these flowers, and the black *vomito* ; reptiles trail at your feet. If you gave way to fatigue, a noiseless army of implacable anatomists would take possession of you, and with a million lancets convert all your tissues into an admirable bit of lacework, a gauze veil, a breath, nothingness.

To this all-absorbing abyss of devouring death, of famished life, what does God oppose to re-assure us ? Another abyss, not less famished, thirsty of life, but less implacable to man. I see the Bird, and I breathe !

What ! is it in ye, bright living flowers ! ye winged topazes and sapphires, that I shall find my safety ? Your saving vehemence it is, stimulated for the purification of this superabundant and furious fecundity, that alone renders practicable the entrance to this danger-ous realm of faëry. Were you absent, jealous Nature would perform her mysterious labour of solitary fermentation, and not even the most daring savant would venture upon observing her. Who am I here ? And how shall I defend myself ? What power would be sufficient ?

The elephant, the ancient mammoth, would perish defenceless against a million of deadly darts.   Who will brave them !   The eagle or the condor ?   No; a people far more mighty—the intrepid and the innumerable legion of fly-catchers.

Humming-birds, colibris, and their brothers of every hue, live with impunity in these gleaming solitudes where danger lurks on every side ; live among the most venomous insects, and upon those mournful plants whose very shadow kills.   One of them (crested, green and blue), in the Antilles, suspends his nest to the most terrible and fatal of trees, to the spectre whose fatal glance seems to freeze your blood for ever, to the deadly manchineal.

Wonder of wonders !   It is this parroquet which boldly crops the fruits of the fearful tree, feeds upon them, assumes their livery, and appears, from his sinister green, to draw the metallic lustre of his triumphant wings.

Life in these winged flames, the humming-bird and the colibri, is so glowing, so intense, that it scorns every poison.   They beat their wings with such swiftness that the eye cannot count the pulsations ; yet, meanwhile, the bird seems motionless, completely inert and inactive. He maintains a continual cry of *hour! hour!* until, with bended head, he plunges the dagger of his beak into the depth of the flowers, exhausting their sweets and the tiny insects among them; all, too, with a motion so rapid that nothing can be compared to it—a sharp, choleric, extremely impatient motion, sometimes transported by fury—against what? against a great bird, which he pursues and hunts to the death; against an already rifled blossom, which he cannot forgive for not having waited for him. He rends it, devastates it, and scatters abroad its petals.

Leaves, as we know, absorb the poisons in the atmosphere; flowers exhale them. These birds live upon flowers, upon these pungent flowers, on their sharp and burning juices, in a word, on poisons. From their acids they seem to derive their sharp cry and the everlasting agitation of their angry movements. These contribute, and perhaps much more directly than light, to enrich them with those strange reflects which set one thinking of steel, gold, precious stones, rather than of plumage or blossoms.

The contrast between them and man is singular. The latter, throughout these regions, perishes or decays. Europeans who, on the borders of these forests, attempt the cultivation of the cacao and other colonial products, quickly succumb. The natives languish, enfeebled and attenuated. That part of earth where man sinks nearest the level of the beast is the scene of triumph of the bird, where his extraordinary pomp of attire, luxurious and superabundant, has justly won for him the name of bird of paradise.

It matters not! Whatever their plumage, their hues, their forms, this great winged populace, the conquerors and devourers of insects, and, in their stronger species, the eager hunters of reptiles, sweep over all the land as man's pioneers, purifying and making ready his abode. They swim intrepidly on this vast sea of death—this hissing, croaking, crawling sea—on the terrible miasmatic vapours, inhaling and defying them.

It is thus that the great sanitary work, the time-old combat of the bird against the inferior tribes which might long render the

world uninhabitable by man, is continued throughout the earth. Quadrupeds, and even man, take in it but a feeble part. It is ever the war of the winged Hercules.

To him, indeed, inhabited regions owe all their security. In the furthest Africa, at the Cape, the good serpent-eater defends man against the reptiles. Peaceable in disposition and gentle in aspect, he seems to engage without passion in his dangerous encounters. The gigantic *jabiru* does not labour less in the deserts of Guiana, where man as yet ventures not to live. Their perilous savannahs, alternately inundated and parched, a dubious ocean teeming in the sunshine with a horrible population of monsters as yet unknown, possess, as their superior inhabitant, their intrepid scavenger, a noble bird of battle, retaining some relics of the ancient weapons with which the primeval birds were very probably provided in their struggle against the dragon. These are a horn on the head, and a spur on each of the wings. With the first it stirs up, excites, and rouses out of the mud its enemy. The others serve as a guard and defence : the reptile

which hugs and folds it in its embrace, at the
same time plunges into its own body these keen
darts, and by its constriction, its own actual
exertions, is poniarded.

This brave and beautiful bird, last-born of
the ancient worlds and a surviving witness to forgotten
encounters, which is born, lives, and dies in the slime,
in the primitive cloaca, bears no stain nevertheless of
his unclean cradle. I know not what moral instinct
raises and supports him above it. His grand and
formidable voice, which sways the desert, announces from
afar the gravity and dignified heroism of the noble and
haughty purifier. The kamichi (*Palamedéa cornuta*),
as he is called, is rare ; he forms a genus of himself,
a species which is not divided.

Despising the ignoble promiscuousness of the low
world in which he lives, he lives alone, with but one
mate. Undoubtedly, in his career of war, his mate is
also a companion-in-arms. They love, they fight together ; they follow the same destiny. Theirs is that
soldierly marriage of which Tacitus speaks : " *Sic vivendum, sic
pereundum,*" — " To life, to death." When this tender com-

panionship, this consoling succour, fails the kamichi, he disdains to protract his existence; he rejoins the loved one which he cannot survive.

PURIFICATION.

PURIFICATION.

In the morning—not at the first blush of dawn, but when the sun already mounts the horizon—and at the very moment when the cocoa-nut tree unfolds its leaves, the *urubus* (or little vultures), perched in knots of forty or fifty upon its branches, open their brilliant ruby eyes. The toils of the day demand them. In indolent Africa a hundred villages invoke them; in drowsy America, south of Panama or Caraccas, they, swiftest of cleansers, must sweep out and purify the town before the Spaniard rises, before the potent sun has stirred the scattered carcasses and the heaps of rottenness into fermentation. If they failed a single day, the country would become a desert.

When it is evening-time in America—when the urubu, his day's work ended, replaces himself on the cocoa-nut tree—the minarets of

Asia sparkle in the morning's rays. Not less punctual than their American brothers, vultures, crows, storks, ibises, set out from their balconies on their various missions : some to the fields, to destroy the insect and the serpent; others, alighting in the streets of Alexandria or Cairo, hasten to accomplish their task of municipal scavengering. Did they but take the briefest holiday the plague would soon be the only inhabitant of the country.

Thus, in the two hemispheres, the great work of public health is performed with solemn and wonderful regularity. If the sun is punctual in fertilizing life, these scavengers—sworn in and licensed by nature—are no less punctual in withdrawing from his rays the shocking spectacle of death.

Seemingly they are not ignorant of the importance of their functions. Approach them, and they will not retreat. When they have received the signal from their comrades the crows, which often precede

them and point out their prey, you will see the vultures descend in a cloud from one knows not whence, as if from heaven ! Naturally

solitary, and without communication—mostly silent—they flock to
the banquet by the hundred, and nothing disturbs them. They
quarrel not among themselves, they take no heed of the passer-by.
They imperturbably accomplish their functions in a stern kind of
gravity; with decency and propriety; the corpse disappears, the skin
remains. In a moment a frightful mass of putrid fermentation, which
man had never dared to draw near, has vanished—has re-entered the
pure and wholesome current of universal life.

It is strange that the more useful they are to us, the more odious
we find them. We are unwilling to accept them for what they are,
to regard them in their true *rôle*, as the beneficent crucibles of living
fire through which nature passes everything that might corrupt the
higher life. For this purpose she has provided them with an admirable apparatus, which receives, destroys, transforms, without ever
rejecting, wearying, or even satisfying itself. Let them devour a
hippopotamus, and they are still famished. To the gulls (those
vultures of the sea) a whale seems but a reasonable morsel! They
will dissect it and clear it away more thoroughly than the most skilful whalers. As long as aught of it remains they remain; fire at
them, and they intrepidly return to it in the mouth of your guns.
Nothing dislodges the vulture from the carcass of a hippopotamus.
Levaillant killed one of these birds, which, though mortally wounded,
still plucked away scraps of flesh. Was he starving? Not he; food
was found in his stomach weighing six pounds!

This is automatic gluttony, rather than ferocity. If their aspect
is sad and sombre, nature has favoured them for the most part with a
delicate and feminine ornament, the soft white down about their
neck.

Standing before them, you feel yourself in the presence of the
ministers of death; but of death tranquil and natural, and not of
murder. Like the elements, they are serious, grave, inaccusable, at
bottom innocent—rather, let us say, deserving. Though gifted with
a vital force which resumes, subdues, and absorbs everything, they are
subject, more than any other beings, to general influences; are swayed

by the conditions of atmosphere and temperature; essentially hygro-metrical, they are living barometers. The morning's humidity burdens their heavy wings; the weakest prey at that hour might pass with impunity before them. So great is their subjection to external nature, that the American species, perched in uniform ranks on the cocoa-nut branches, follow, as we have said, the exact hour when the leaves fold up, retire to rest long before evening, and only awake when the sun, already high above the horizon, re-opens the leaves of the tree and their white, heavy eyelids.

These admirable agents of that beneficent chemistry which preserves and balances life here below, labour for us in a thousand places where we ourselves may never penetrate. We clearly discern their presence and their services in our towns; but no one can measure the full extent of their benefits in those deserts where every breath of the winds is death. In the fathomless forest, in the deep morasses, under the impure shadow of mangoes and mangroves, where ferment the corpses of two worlds, dashed to and fro by the sea, the great purify-ing army seconds and shortens the action both of the waves and the insects. Woe to the inhabited world, if their mysterious and unknown toil ceased but for an instant!

In America these public benefactors are protected by the law.

Egypt does more for them; she reveres, she loves them. If the ancient worship no longer exists, they receive from men as kindly an hospitality as in the time of Pharaoh. Ask an Egyptian fellah why he allows himself to be infested and deafened by birds? why he so patiently endures the insolence of the crow posted on his buffalo's horn or his camel's hump, or gathering on the date-palms in flocks and beating down the fruit?—he will answer nothing. To the bird everything is lawful. Older than the Pyramids, he is the ancient inhabitant of the country. Man is there only through his instrument-ality; he could not exist without the persistent toil of the ibis, the stork, the crow, and the vulture.

Hence arises an universal sympathy for the animal, an instinctive tenderness for all life, which, more than anything else, makes the charm of the East. The West has its peculiar splendours—in sun and climate America is not less dazzling; but the moral attraction of Asia lies in the sentiment of unity which you feel in a world where man is not divorced from nature; where the primitive alliance remains unbroken; where the animals are ignorant that they have cause to dread the human species. Laugh at it if you will; but there is a gentle pleasure in observing this confidence—in seeing the birds come at the Brahmin's call to eat from his very hand—in watching the apes on the pagoda-roofs sleeping in domestic peace, playing with or suckling their little ones in as much security as in the bosom of their native forests.

"At Cairo," remarks a traveller, "the turtle-doves know so well

they are under the protection of the public, that they live in the midst of the very clamour of the city. Every day I see them cooing on my window-shutters, in a very narrow street, at the entrance of a noisy bazaar, and at the busiest moment of the year, a little before the Ramadan, when the ceremonies of marriage fill the city day and night with uproar and tumult. The level roofs of the houses, the usual promenade of the prisoners of the harem and their slaves, are in like manner haunted by a crowd of birds. The eagles sleep in confidence on the balconies of the minarets."

Conquerors have never failed to turn into derision this gentleness, this tenderness for animated nature. The Persians, the Romans in Egypt, our Europeans in India, the French in Algeria, have often outraged and stricken these innocent brothers of man, the object of his ancient reverence. A Cambyses slew the sacred cow; a Roman the ibis or cat which destroyed unclean reptiles. But what means the cow? The fecundity of the country. And the ibis? Its salubrity. Destroy these animals, and the country is no longer habitable. That which has saved India and Egypt through so many misfortunes, and preserved their fertility, is neither the Nile nor the Ganges; it is respect for animal life, the mildness and the gentle heart of man.

Profound in meaning was the speech of the priest of Saïs to the Greek Herodotus: "You shall be children ever."

We shall always be so—we, men of the West—subtle and graceful reasoners, so long as we shall not have comprehended, with a simple and more exhaustive view, the *motive* of things. To be a child is to seize life only by partial glimpses. To be a man is to be fully conscious of all its harmonious unity. The child disports himself, shatters, and destroys; he finds his happiness in undoing. And science in its childhood does the same; it cannot study unless it kills; the sole use which it makes of a living miracle is, in the first place, to dissect it. None of us carry into our scientific pursuits that tender reverence for life which nature rewards by unveiling to us her mysteries.

Enter the catacombs, where, to employ our haughty language, the rude monuments sleep of a barbarous superstition; visit the treasure-stores of India and Egypt; at each step you meet with naïve but not the less profound intuitions of the essential mystery of life and death.

Do not let the form deceive you; do not look upon this as an artificial work, fabricated by a priestly hand. Under the strange complexity and burdensome tyranny of the sacerdotal form, I see two sentiments everywhere revealing themselves in a human and pathetic manner :—

The effort to save the loved soul from the shipwreck of death ;

The tender brotherhood of man and nature, the religious sympathy for the dumb animal as the divine instrument in the protection of human life.

The instinct of antiquity perceived what observation and science declare: that the Bird is the agent of the grand universal transition, and of purification—the wholesome accelerator of the interchange of substances. Especially in burning countries, where every delay is a peril, he is, as Egypt said, the barque of safety which receives the dead spoil, and causes it to re-enter the domain of life and the world of purity.

The fond and grateful Egyptian soul has recognized these benefits, and wishes for no happiness which it cannot share with the animals, its benefactors. It does not desire to be saved alone. It endeavours to associate them in its immortality. It wills that the sacred bird accompany it to the sombre realm, as if to bear it on its wings.

DEATH.

DEATH.

BIRDS OF PREY.—(THE RAPTORES).

It was one of my saddest hours when, seeking in nature a refuge from the thoughts of the age, I for the first time encountered the head of the viper. This occurred in a valuable museum of anatomical imitations. The head, marvellously imitated and enormously enlarged, so as to remind one of the tiger's and the jaguar's, exposed in its horrible form a something still more horrible. You seized at once the delicate, infinite, fearfully prescient precautions by which the deadly machine is so potently armed. Not only is it provided with numerous keen-edged teeth; not only are these teeth supplied with an ingenious reservoir of poison which slays immediately; but their extreme fineness, which renders them liable to fracture, is compensated by an advantage that perhaps no other animal possesses; namely, a magazine of super-numerary teeth, to supply at need the place of any accidentally broken. Oh, what provisions for killing! What precautions that the victim shall not escape! What love for this horrible creature! I stood by it *scandalized*, if I may so speak, and with a sick soul. Nature, the great mother, by whose side I had taken refuge, shocked me with a maternity so cruelly impartial.

Gloomily I walked away, bearing on my heart a darker shadow than rested on the day itself, one of the sternest in winter. I had come forth like a child; I returned home like an orphan, feeling the notion of a Providence dying away within me.

Our impressions are not less painful when we see in our galleries the endless series of birds of prey, prowlers by day and night, frightful masks of birds, phantoms which terrify the day itself. One is powerfully affected by observing their cruel weapons; I do not

refer to those terrible beaks which kill with a blow, but those talons, those sharpened saws, those instruments of torture which fix the shuddering prey, protract the last keen pangs and the agony of suffering.

Ah! our globe is a barbarous world, though still in its youth; a world of attempts and rude beginnings, given over to cruel slaveries— to night, hunger, death, fear! Death? We can accept it; there is in the soul enough of hope and faith to look upon it as a passage, a stage of initiation, a gate to better worlds. But, alas, was pain so useful as to render it necessary to prodigalize it? I feel it, I see it, I hear it everywhere. Not to hear it, to preserve the thread of my thoughts, I am forced to stop up my ears. All the activity of my soul would be suspended, my nerves shattered by it; I should effect nothing more, I should no longer move forward; my life and powers of production would remain barren, annihilated by pity!

"And yet is not pain the warning which teaches us to foresee and to anticipate, and by every means in our power to ward off our dissolution? This cruel school is the stimulant and spur of prudence for all living things—a powerful drawing back of the soul upon itself, which otherwise would be enfeebled by happiness, by soft and weakening impressions.

"May it not be said that happiness has a centrifugal attraction which diffuses us wholly without, detains us, dissipates us, would evaporate and restore us to the elements, if we wholly abandoned ourselves to it? Pain, on the contrary, if experienced at one point, brings back all to the centre, knits closer, prolongs, ensures and fortifies existence.

"Pain is in some wise the artist of the world which creates us, fashions us, sculptures us with the fine edge of a pitiless chisel. It limits the overflowing life. And that which remains, stronger and more exquisite, enriched by its very loss, draws thence the gift of a higher being."

These thoughts of resignation were awakened by one who was herself a sufferer, and whose clear eye discerned, even before I myself did, my troubles and my doubts.

As the individual, said she again, so is the world. Earth itself has been benefited by Pain. Nature begot her through the violent

action of these ministers of death. Their species, rapidly growing
rarer and rarer, are the memorials, the evidences of an anterior stage
of the globe in which the inferior life swarmed, while nature laboured
to purge the excessive fecundity.

We can retrace in thought the scale of the successive necessities
of destruction which the earth was thus constrained to undergo.

Against the irrespirable air which at first enveloped it, vegetables
were its saviours.   Against the suffocating and terrific density of
these lower vegetable forms, the rough coating which encrusted it,
the nibbling, gnawing insect, which we have since execrated, was the
sanitary agent.   Against the insect, the frog, and the reptile mass,
the venomous reptile proved an useful expurgator.   Finally, when
the higher life, the winged life, took its flight, earth found a barrier
against the too rapid transports of her young fecundity in the powerful voracious birds, eagles, falcons, or vultures.

But these useful destroyers have diminished in numbers as they
have become less necessary.   The swarms of small creeping animals
on which the viper principally whetted his teeth having wonderfully
thinned, the viper also grows rare.   The world of winged game being
cleared in its turn, either by man's depredations or by the disappearance of certain insects on which the small birds lived, you see that

the odious tyrants of the air are also decreasing; the eagle is seldom
met with, even among the Alps, and the exaggerated and enor-

mous prices which the falcon fetches, seems to prove that the former, the noblest of the raptores, has now-a-days nearly disappeared.

Thus nature gravitates towards a less violent order. Does this mean that death will ever diminish? Death! no; but pain surely.

The world little by little falls under the power of the Being who alone understands the useful equilibrium of life and death, who can regulate it in such wise as to maintain the scale even between the living species, and encourage them according to their merit or innocence—to simplify, to soften, and (if I may hazard the word) to moralize death, by rending it swift, and freeing it from anguish.

Death was never our serious objection. Is it more than a simple mask of life's transformations? But pain is an objection, grave, cruel, terrible. Therefore, little by little, it will disappear from the earth. Its agents, the fierce executioners of the life which they plucked out by torture, are already very rare.

Assuredly, when I survey, in the Museum, the sinister assemblage of nocturnal and diurnal birds of prey, I do not much regret the destruction of these species. Whatever pleasure our personal instincts of violence, our admiration of strength, may cause us to take in these winged robbers, it is impossible to misread in their deathlike masks the baseness of their nature. Their pitifully flattened skulls are sufficient evidence that, though greatly favoured with wing, and crooked beak, and talons, they have not the least need to make use of their intelligence. Their constitution, which has made them swiftest of the swift, strongest of the strong, has enabled them to dispense with address, stratagem, and tactic. As for the courage with which one is tempted to endow them, what occasion have they to display it, since they encounter none but inferior enemies? Enemies? no; victims! When the rigour of the season, or hunger, drives their young to emigrate, it leads to the beak of these dull tyrants countless numbers of innocents, very superior in every sense to their murderers; it prodigalizes the birds which are artists, and singers, and architects, as a prey to these vulgar assassins; and for the eagle and the buzzard provides a banquet of nightingales.

The flattened skull is the degrading sign of these murderers. I trace it in the most extolled, in those whom man has the most flattered, and even in the noble falcon; noble, it is true, and I the less dispute the justice of the title, because, unlike the eagle and other executioners, it knows how to kill its prey at a blow, and scorns to torture it.

These birds of prey, with their small brains, offer a striking contrast to the numerous amiable and plainly intelligent species which we find among the smaller birds. The head of the former is only a beak; that of the latter has a face. What comparison can be made between these brute giants and the intelligent, all-human bird, the robin redbreast, which at this very moment hovers about me, perches on my shoulder or my paper, examines my writing, warms himself at the fire, or curiously peers through the window to see if the spring-time will not soon return.

If there be any choice among the raptores, I should certainly prefer—dare I say it?—the vulture to the eagle. Among the bird-world I have seen nothing so grand, so imposing, as our five Algerian vultures (in the Jardin des Plantes), posted together like so many Turkish pachas, adorned with superb cravats of the most delicate white down, and draped in noble mantles of gray. A solemn divan of exiles, who seem to discuss among themselves the vicissitudes of things and the political events which have driven them from their native country.

What real difference exists between the eagle and the vulture? The eagle passionately loves blood, and prefers living flesh, very rarely eating the dead. The vulture seldom kills, and directly benefits life by restoring to its service, and to the grand current of vital circulation, the disorganized objects which others could only assimilate to their disorganization. The eagle lives upon murder only, and may justly be entitled the minister of Death. On the contrary, the vulture is the servant of Life.

Owing to his strength and beauty, the eagle has been adopted as an emblem by more than one warrior race which lived, like himself, by rapine. The Persians and the Romans chose him. We now associate him with the lofty ideas which these great empires originate. Grave people—even an Aristotle—have accredited the absurd fable that he daringly eyed the sun, and put his offspring to the test, by making them also gaze upon it. Once started on this glorious road, the philosophers halted no more. Buffon went the furthest. He eulogizes the eagle for his *temperance*. He does not eat at all, says he. The truth is, that when his prey is large, he feasts himself on the spot,

and carries but a small portion to his family. The king of the air, says he again, *disdains small animals*. But observation points to a directly opposite conclusion. The ordinary eagle attacks with eagerness the most timid of beings, the hare; the spotted eagle assails the duck. The booted eagle has a preference for field mice and house mice, and eats them so greedily that he swallows them without killing them. The bald-headed eagle, or pygargo, will frequently slay her own young, and often drives them from her nest before they can support themselves.

Near Havre I have observed one instance of truly royal nobility, and, above all, of sobriety, in an eagle. A bird, captured at sea, but which has fallen into far too kindly hands in a butcher's house, is so gorged with an abundance of food obtained without fighting, that he appears to regret nothing. A Falstaff of an eagle, he grows fat, and cares no longer for the chase, or the plains of heaven. If he no longer fixedly eyes the sun, he watches the kitchen, and for a titbit allows the children to drag him by the tail.

If rank is to be decided by strength, the first place must not be given to the eagle, but to the bird which figures in the "Thousand and One Nights" under the name of *Roc*, the condor, the giant of gigantic mountains, the Cordilleras. It is the largest of the vultures—is, fortunately, the rarest—and the most destructive, as it feeds only on live prey. When it meets with a large animal, it so gorges itself with meat that it is unable to stir, and may then be killed with a few blows of a stick.

To judge these species truly we must examine the eyrie of the eagle, the rude, ill-constructed platform which serves for its nest; compare this rough and clumsy work—I do not say with the delicate *chef-d'œuvre* of a chaffinch's nest—but with the constructions of insects, the excavations of ants, where the industrious workman varies his art to infinity, and displays a genius so singular in its foresight and resources.

The traditional esteem which man cherishes for the courage of the great Raptores is much diminished when we read, in Wilson, that a tiny bird, a fly-catcher, such as the purple martin, will hunt the great black eagle, pursue it, harass it, banish it from its district, give it not a moment's repose. It is a truly extraordinary spectacle to see this little hero, adding all his weight to his strength, that he may make the greater impression, rise and let himself drop from the clouds on the back of the large robber, mount without letting go, and prick him forward with his beak in lieu of a spur.

Without going so far as America, you may see, in the Jardin des Plantes, the ascendancy of the little over the great, of mind over matter, in the singular tête-à-tête of the gypaetus and the crow. The latter, a very feeble animal, and the feeblest of birds of prey, which in his black garb has the air of a pedagogue, labours hard to civilize his brutal fellow-prisoner, the gypaetus. It is amusing to observe how he teaches him to play—humanizes him, so to speak—by a hundred tricks of his own invention, and refines his rude nature. This comedy is performed with special distinction when the crow has a reasonable number of spectators. It has appeared to me that he disdains to exhibit his *savoir-faire* before a single eye-witness. He calculates upon their assistance, earns their respect in case of need. I have seen him dart back with his beak the little pebbles which a child had flung at him. The most remarkable pastime which he teaches to his big friend is, to make him hold by one end a stick which he himself draws by the other. This show of a struggle between strength and weakness, this simulated equality, is well adapted to soften the barbarian, and though at first he gives but little heed to it, he afterwards yields to continued urgency, and ends by throwing himself into the sport with a savage good temper.

In the presence of this repulsively ferocious figure, armed with invincible talons and a beak tipped with iron, which would kill at the first blow, the crow has not the least fear. With the security of a superior mind, before this heavy mass he goes, he comes, he wheels

about, he snatches its prey before its eyes; the other growls, but too late; his tutor, far more nimble, with his black eye, metallic and lustrous as steel, has seen the forward movement; he leaps away; if need be, he climbs a branch or two higher; he growls in his turn— he admonishes his companion.

This facetious personage has in his pleasantry the advantage due to the seriousness, gravity, and sadness of his demeanour. I saw one daily, in the streets of Nantes, on the threshold of an alley, which, in his demi-captivity, could only console himself for his clipped wings by playing tricks with the dogs. He suffered the curs to pass unmolested ; but when his malicious eye espied a dog of handsome

figure, worthy indeed of his courage, he hopped behind him, and, by a skilful and unperceived manœuvre, leapt upon his back, gave him, hot and dry, two stabs with his strong black beak: the dog fled, howling. Satisfied, tranquil, and serious, the crow returned to his post, and one could never have supposed that so grim-looking a fellow had just indulged in such an escapade.

It is said that in a state of freedom, strong in his spirit of association, and in his numbers, he hazards the most audacious games, even to watching the absence of the eagle, stealing into his redoubtable nest, and robbing it of the eggs. And, what is more difficult to believe, naturalists pretend to have seen great troops of crows, which, when the eagle is at home, and defending his family, deafen him with their cries, defy him, entice him forth, and contrive, though not without a battle, to carry off an eaglet.

Such exertions and such danger for this miserable prey! If the thing be true, we must suppose that the prudent republic, frequently troubled or harassed by the tyrant of the country, decrees the extinction of his race, and believes itself bound by a great act of devotion, cost what it may, to execute the decree.

Their sagacity is shown in a thousand ways, especially in the judicious and well-weighed choice of their abode. Those which I observed at Nantes, on one of the hills of the Erdre, passed over my head every morning, and returned every evening. Evidently they had their town and country houses. By day they perched on the cathedral towers to make their observations, ferreting out (*éventant*) what good things the city might have to offer. At close of day, they regained the woods, and the well-sheltered rocks where they love to pass the night. These are domiciliated people, and no mere birds of passage. Attached to their family, especially to their mates, to whom they are scrupulously loyal, their peculiar dwelling-place should be the nest. But the dread of the great birds of night decides them to sleep together in twenties or thirties—a sufficient number for a combat, if

such should arise. Their special object of hate and horror is the owl; when day breaks, they take their revenge for his nocturnal misdeeds:

they hoot him; they give him chase; profiting by his embarrassment, they persecute him to death.

There is no form of association by which they do not know how to profit. That which is sweetest—the family—does not induce them to forget, as you may see, the confederacy for defence or the league for attack. On the contrary, they associate themselves even with their superior rivals, the vultures, and call, precede, or follow them, to feed at their expense. They unite—and this is a stronger illustration—with their enemy the eagle; at least, they surround him to profit by his combats, by the fray in which he triumphs over some great animal. These shrewd spectators wait at a little distance until the eagle has feasted to his satisfaction, and gorged himself with blood; when this takes place, he flies away, and the remainder falls to the crows.

Their evident superiority over so great a number of birds is due to their longevity, and to the experience which their excellent memory enables them to acquire and profit by. Very different from the majority of animals, whose duration of life is proportionable to the duration of their infancy, they reach maturity at the end of a year, and live, it is said, a century.

The great variety of their food, which includes every kind of animal or vegetable nutriment, every dead or living prey, gives them a wide acquaintance with things and seasons, harvests and hunts. They interest themselves in everything, and observe everything. The ancients, who lived far more completely than ourselves in and with nature, found it no small profit to follow, in a hundred obscure things where human experience as yet affords no light, the directions of so prudent and sage a bird.

With due submission to the noble Raptores, the crow, which frequently guides them, despite his "inky suit" and uncouth visage, despite the coarseness of appetite imputed to him, is not the less the superior genius of the great species of which he is, in size, already a diminution.

But the crow, after all, represents only utilitarian prudence, the

wisdom of self-interest.   To arrive at the higher orders, the heroes of
the winged race, the sublime and impassioned artists, we must reduce
the bird in size, and lower the material to exalt the mental and moral
development.   Nature, like so many mothers, has shown a weakness
for her smallest offspring.

Part Second.

THE LIGHT—THE NIGHT.

THE LIGHT.

THE NIGHT.

"LIGHT! more light!" Such were the last words of Goethe. This utterance of expiring genius is the general cry of Nature, and re-echoes from world to world. What was said by that man of power—one of the eldest sons of God—is said by His humblest children, the least advanced in the scale of animal life, the molluscs in the depths of ocean; they will not dwell where the light never penetrates. The flower seeks the beam, turns towards it; without it, sickens. Our fellow-workers, the animals, rejoice like us, or mourn like us, according as it comes or goes. My grandson, but two months old, bursts into tears when the day declines.

"This summer, when walking in my garden, I heard and I saw on a branch a bird singing to the setting sun; he inclined himself towards its rays, and was plainly enchanted by it. I was equally charmed to see him; our pitiful caged birds had never inspired me with the idea of that intelligent and powerful creature, so little, so full of passion. I trembled at his song. He bent his head behind him, his bosom swelled; never singer or poet enjoyed so simple an ecstasy. It was not love, however (the season was past); it was clearly the glory of the day which raptured him—the charm of the gentle sun!

"Barbarous is the science, the hard pride, which disparages to such an extent animated nature, and raises so impassable a barrier between man and his inferior brothers!

"With tears I said to him: 'Poor child of light, which thou reflectest in thy song, truly thou hast good cause to hymn it! Night, replete with snares and dangers for thee, too closely resembles death. Would that thou mightst see the light of the morrow!' Then, passing in spirit from *his* destiny to that of all living beings which, since the dim profundities of creation, have so slowly risen to the day, I said, like Goethe and the little bird: 'Light, light, O Lord, more light!'"
—(MICHELET, *The People*, p. 62, edit. 1846.)

The world of fishes is the world of silence. Men say, "Dumb as a fish."

The world of insects is the world of night. They are all light-shunners. Even those, which, like the bee, labour during the day-time, prefer the shades of obscurity.

The world of birds is the world of light—of song.

All of them live in the sun, fill themselves with it, or are inspired by it. Those of the South carry its reflected radiance on their wings; those of our colder climates in their songs; many of them follow it from land to land.

"See," says St. John, "how at morning time they hail the rising sun, and at evening faithfully congregate to watch it setting on our Scottish shores. Towards evening, the heath-cock, that he may see it longer, stands on tiptoe and balances himself on the branch of the tallest willow."

Light, love, and song, have for them but one meaning. If you would have the captive nightingale sing when it is not the season of his loves, cover up his cage, then suddenly let in the light upon him, and he recovers his voice. The unfortunate chaffinch, blinded by barbarous hands, sings with a despairing and sickly animation, creating for himself the light of harmony with his voice, becoming a sun unto himself in his internal fire.

I would willingly believe that this is the chief inspiration of the bird's song in our gloomy climates, where the sun appears only in vivid flashes. In comparison with those brilliant zones where he never quits the horizon, our countries, veiled in mist and cloud, but glowing at intervals, have exactly the effect of the cage, first covered, and then exposed, of the imprisoned nightingale. They provoke the strain, and, like light, awaken bursts of harmony.

Even the bird's flight is influenced by it.   Flight depends on the eye quite as much as on the wing.　Among species gifted with a keen and delicate vision, like the falcon, which from the loftiest heights of heaven can espy the wren in a thicket—like the swallow, which, from a distance of one thousand feet, can perceive a gnat—flight is sure, daring, and charming to look at in its infallible certainty.　Far otherwise is it with the myopes, the short-sighted, as you may see by their gait; they fly with caution, grope about, and are afraid of falling.

The eye and the wing—sight and flight—that exalted degree of puissance which ever enables you to embrace in a sudden glance, and to range over kingdoms, vast countries, immense landscapes—which permits you to see in complete detail, and not to contract, as in a geographical chart, so grand a variety of objects—to possess and to discern, almost as if you were the equal of God;—oh, what a source of boundless enjoyment! what a strange and mysterious happiness, scarcely conceivable by man!

Observe, too, these perceptions are so strong and so vivid that they grave themselves on the memory, and to such a degree that even an inferior animal like a pigeon retraces and recognizes every little *accident* in a road which he has traversed only once.　How, then, will it be with the sage stork, the shrewd crow, the intelligent swallow?

Let us confess this superiority.　Let us regard without envy those blisses of vision which may, perhaps, one day be ours in a happier existence.　This felicity of seeing so much—of seeing so far—of seeing so clearly—of piercing the infinite with the eye and the wing, almost at the same moment,—to what does it belong?　To that life which is our distant ideal.　*A life in the fulness of light, and without shadow!*

Already the bird's existence is, as it were, a foretaste of it.　It would here prove to him a divine source of knowledge, if, in its sublime freedom, it were not burdened by the two fatalities which chain our globe to a condition of barbarism, and render futile all our aspirations.

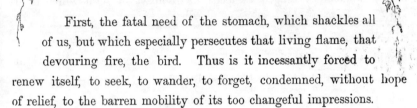

First, the fatal need of the stomach, which shackles all of us, but which especially persecutes that living flame, that devouring fire, the bird.   Thus is it incessantly forced to renew itself, to seek, to wander, to forget, condemned, without hope of relief, to the barren mobility of its too changeful impressions.

The other fatal necessity is that of night, of slumber, hours of shadow and ambush, when his wing is broken or captured, or, while defenceless, he loses the power of flight, strength, and light.

When we speak of light, we mean safety for all creatures.

It is the guarantee of life for man and the animal ; it is, as it were, the serene, calm, and reassuring smile, the privilege of Nature. It puts an end to the sombre terrors which pursue us in the shadows, to the not unfounded fears, and to the torment also of cruel dreams— to the troublous thoughts which agitate and overthrow the soul.

In the security of civil association which has existed for so long a period, man can scarcely comprehend the agonies of savage life during the hours that Nature leaves it defenceless, when her terrible impartiality opens the way to death no less legitimate than life.   In vain you reproach her.   She tells the bird that the owl also has a right to live.   She replies to man : "I must feed my lions."

Read in books of travels the panic of unfortunate castaways lost in the solitudes of Africa, of the miserable fugitive slave who escapes the barbarity of man only to fall into the hands of a barbarous nature.   What tortures, as soon as at sunset the lion's ill-omened scouts, the wolves and jackals, begin to prowl, accompanying him at a distance, preceding him to scent his prey, or following him like ghouls !   They whine in your ears : "To-morrow we shall seek thy bones !"   But, O horror ! see here, at but two paces distant !   He

sees you, watches you, sends a deep roar from the cavernous recesses
of his throat of brass, sums up his living prey, exacts and lays claim
to it! The horse cannot be held still; he trembles, a cold sweat
pours over him, he plunges to and fro. His rider, crouching between
the watch-fires, if he succeeds in kindling any, with difficulty preserves sufficient strength to feed the rampart of light which is his
only safeguard.

Night is equally terrible for the birds, even in our climates, where it
would seem less dangerous. What monsters it conceals, what frightful chances for the bird lurk in its obscurity! Its nocturnal foes have
this characteristic in common—their approach is noiseless. The
screech-owl flies with a silent wing, as if wrapped in tow (*comme
étoupée de ouate*). The weasel insinuates its long body into the nest
without disturbing a leaf. The eager polecat, athirst for the warm
life-blood, is so rapid, that in a moment it bleeds both parents and progeny, and slaughters a whole family.

It seems that the bird, when it has little ones, enjoys a second
sight for these dangers. It has to protect a family far more feeble
and more helpless than that of the quadruped, whose young can walk
as soon as born. But how protect them? It can do nothing but
remain at its post and die; it cannot fly away, for its love has broken
its wings. All night the narrow entry of the nest is guarded by the
father, who sinks with fatigue, and opposes danger with feeble beak
and shaking head. What will this avail if the enormous jaw of the
serpent suddenly appears, or the horrible eye of the bird of death,
immeasurably enlarged by fear?

Anxious for its young, it has little care for itself. In its season
of solitude Nature spares it the tortures of prevision. Sad and
dejected rather than alarmed, it is silent, it sinks down and hides its
little head under its wings, and even its neck disappears among the
plumes. This position of complete self-abandonment, of confidence,
which it had held in the egg—in the happy maternal prison, where
its security was so perfect—it resumes every evening in the midst of
perils and without protection.

Heavy for all creatures is the gloom of evening, and even for the protected. The Dutch painters have seized and expressed this truth very forcibly in reference to the beasts grazing at liberty in the meadows. The horse of his own accord draws near his companion, and rests his head upon him. The cow, followed by her calf, returns to the fence, and would fain find her way to the byre. For these animals have a stable, a lodging, a shelter against nocturnal snares. The bird has but a leaf for its roof!

How great, then, its happiness in the morning, when terrors vanish, when the shadows fade away, when the smallest coppice brightens and grows clear! What chattering on the edge of every nest, what lively conversations! It is, as it were, a mutual felicitation at seeing one another again, at being still alive! Then the songs commence. From the furrow the lark mounts aloft, with a loud hymn, and bears to heaven's gate the joy of earth.

As with the bird, so with man. Every line in the ancient Vedas of India is a hymn to the light, the guardian of life—to the sun which

every day, by unveiling the world, creates it anew and preserves it.
We revive, we breathe again, we traverse our dwelling-places, we
regain our families, we count over our herds.   Nothing has perished,
and life is complete.   No tiger has surprised us.   No horde of beasts
of prey has invaded us.   The black serpent has not profited by our
slumbers.   Blessed be thou, O sun, who givest us yet another day !

All animals,—says the Hindu,—and especially the wisest, the
elephant, *the Brahmin of creation,*—salute the sun, and praise it
gratefully at dawn ; they sing to it from their own hearts a hymn of
thankfulness.

But a single creature utters it for all of us, and joyously chants the
strain, sings it.   Who ?   One of the weak—which fears most keenly
the night, and hails with eagerest joy the morning—which lives in
and by the light—whose tender, infinitely sensitive, extended, penetrating vision, discerns all its accidents—and which is most intimately
associated with the decline, the eclipses, and the resurrection of light.

The bird for all nature chants a morning hymn and the bene-
diction of the day.   He is her priest and her augur, her divine and
innocent voice.

THE STORM AND THE WINTER—MIGRATIONS.

THE STORM AND THE WINTER.

MIGRATIONS.

ONE of Nature's confidants, a sacred soul, as simple as profound, the poet Virgil, saw in the bird, as the ancient Italian wisdom had seen in it, an augur and a prophet of the changes of the skies :——

" Nul, sans être averti, n'éprouva les orages—
　　La grue, avec effroi, s'élançant des vallées,
　　Fuit ces noires vapeurs de la terre exhalées—
　　L'hirondelle en volant effleure le rivage;
　　Tremblante pour ses œufs, la fourmi déménage.
　　Des lugubres corbeaux les noires légions
　　Fendent l'air, qui frémit sous leurs longs bataillons—
　　Vois les oiseaux de mer, et ceux que les prairies
　　Nourrissent près des eaux sur des rives fleuries.
　　De leur séjour humide on les voit s'approcher,
　　Offrir leur tête aux flots qui battent le rocher,
　　Promener sur les eaux leur troupe vagabonde,
　　Se plonger dans leur sein, reparaître sur l'onde,
　　S'y replonger encore, et, par cent jeux divers,
　　Annoncer les torrents suspendus dans les airs.
　　Seule, errante à pas lents sur l'aride rivage.
　　La corneille enrouée appelle aussi l'orage.

Le soir, la jeune fille, en tournant son fuseau,
Tire encore de sa lampe un présage nouveau,
Lorsque la mèche en feu, dont la clarté s'émousse,
Se couvre en petillant de noirs flocons de mousse.

*   *   *   *   *

Mais la sécurité reparaît à son tour—
L'alcyon ne vient plus sur l'humide rivage,
Aux tiédeurs du soleil étaler son plumage—
L'air s'éclaircit enfin ; du sommet des montagnes,
Le brouillard affaissé descend dans les campagnes,
Et le triste hibou, le soir, au haut des toits,
En longs gémissements ne traîne plus sa voix.
Les corbeaux même, instruits de la fin de l'orage,
Folâtrent à l'envi parmi l'épais feuillage,
Et, d'un gosier moins rauque, annonçant les beaux jours,
Vont revoir dans leurs nids le fruit de leurs amours."

" *The Georgics," translated by Delille.**

A being eminently electrical, the bird is more *en rapport* than any other with numerous meteorological phenomena of heat and magnetism, whose secrets neither our senses nor our appreciation can arrive at.   He perceives them in their birth, and their early beginnings, even before they manifest themselves.   He possesses, as it were, a kind of physical prescience.   What more natural than that man, whose perception is much slower, and who does not recognize them

---

* We subjoin Dryden's version of the above passage (" *Georgics," Book I.) :—

" Wet weather seldom hurts the most unwise,
So plain the signs, such prophets are the skies :
The wary crane foresees it first, and sails
Above the storm, and leaves the lowly vales ;
The cow looks up, and from afar can find
The change of heaven, and snuffs it in the wind.
The swallow skims the river's watery face,
The frogs renew the croaks of their loquacious race. . . .
Besides, the several sorts of watery fowls,
That swim the seas, or haunt the standing pools ;
The swans that sail along the silver flood,
And dive with stretching necks to search their food,
Then lave their back with sprinkling dews in vain,
And stem the stream to meet the promised rain.
The crow, with clamorous cries, the shower demands,
And single stalks along the desert sands.
The nightly virgin, while her wheel she plies,
Foresees the storm impending in the skies.

until after the event, should interrogate this instructive precursor which announces them ? This is the principle of auguries. And there is no truer wisdom than this pretended " folly of antiquity."

Meteorology, especially, may derive from hence a great advantage, and in it possess the most reliable means. And already it *has* found a guide in the foresight of the birds. Would to Heaven that Napoleon, in September 1811, had taken note of the premature migration of the birds of the North ! From the storks and the cranes he might have secured the most trustworthy information. In their precocious departure, he might have divined the imminency of a severe and terrible winter. They hastened towards the South, and he—he remained at Moscow !

In the midst of the ocean, the weary bird which reposes for a night on the vessel's mast, beguiled afar from his route by this moving asylum, recovers it, nevertheless, without difficulty. So complete is his sympathy with the globe, so exactly does he know the true realm of light, that, on the following morning, he commits himself to the breeze without hesitation ; the briefest con-sultation with himself suffices. He chooses, on the immense abyss, uniform and without other path than the vessel's track, the exact course which will lead him whither he wishes to go. There, not as

When sparkling lamps their sputtering light advance.
And in the sockets oily bubbles dance.
  " Then, after showers, 'tis easy to descry,
Returning suns, and a serener sky;
The stars shine smarter, and the moon adorns,
As with unborrowed beams, her sharpened horns :
The filmy gossamer now flits no more,
Nor halcyons bask on the short sunny shore :
Their litter is not tossed by sows unclean,
But a blue draughty mist descends upon the plain.
And owls, that mark the setting sun, declare
A star-light evening, and a morning fair. . . .
Then thrice the ravens rend the liquid air,
And croaking notes proclaim the settled fair.
Then, round their airy palaces they fly
To greet the sun : and seized with secret joy
When storms are over-blown, with food repair
To their forsaken nests, and callow care."

upon land, exists no local observation, no landmark, no guide; the currents of the atmosphere alone, in sympathy with those of water—perhaps, also, some invisible magnetic currents—pilot this hardy voyager.

How strange a science! Not only does the swallow in Europe know that the insect which fails him there awaits him elsewhere, and goes in quest of it, travelling along the meridian; but in the same latitude, and under the same climates, the loriot of the United States understands that the cherry is ripe in France, and departs without hesitation to gather his harvest of our fruits.

It would be wrong to believe that these migrations occur in their season, without any definite choice of days, and at indeterminate epochs. We ourselves have been able to observe, on the contrary, the exact and lucid decision which regulates them; not an hour too soon or too late.

When living at Nantes, in October 1851, the season being still exceptionally fine, the insects numerous, and the feeding-ground of the swallows plentifully provided, it was our happy chance to catch sight of the sage republic, convoked in one immense and noisy assembly, deliberating on the roof of the church of St. Felix, which dominates over the Erdre, and looks across the Loire. Why was the meeting held on this particular day, at this hour more than at any other? We did not know; soon afterwards we were able to understand it.

Bright was the morning sky, but the wind blew from La Vendée. My pines bewailed their fate, and from my afflicted cedar issued a low deep voice of mourning. The ground was strewn with fruit, which we all set to work to gather.   Gradually the weather grew cloudy, the sky assumed a dull leaden gray, the wind sank, all was death-like.   It was then, at about four o'clock, that simultaneously arrived, from all points, from the wood, from the Erdre, from the city, from the Loire, from the Sèvre, infinite legions, darkening the day, which settled on the church roof, with a myriad voices, a myriad cries, debates, discussions.   Though ignorant of their language, it was not difficult for us to perceive that they differed among themselves. It may be that the youngest, beguiled by the warm breath of autumn, would fain have lingered longer.   But the wiser and more experienced travellers insisted upon departure.   They prevailed; the black masses, moving all at once like a huge cloud, winged their flight towards the south-east, probably towards Italy.   They had scarcely accomplished three hundred leagues (four or five hours' flight) before all the cataracts of heaven were let loose to deluge the earth ; for a moment we thought it was a Flood.   Sheltered in our house, which shook with the furious blast, we admired the wisdom of the winged soothsayers, which had so prudently anticipated the annual epoch of migration.

Clearly it was not hunger that had driven them.   With a beautiful and still abundant nature around them, they had perceived and seized upon the precise hour, without antedating it.   The morrow would have been too late.   The insects, beaten down by the tempest of rain, would have been undiscoverable ; all the life on which they subsisted would have taken refuge in the earth.

Moreover, it is not famine alone, or the forewarning of famine, that decides the movements of the migrating species.   If those birds which live on insects are constrained to depart, those which feed on wild berries might certainly remain.   What impels *them* ? Is it the cold ? Most of them could readily endure it.   To these special reasons we must add another, of a loftier and more general character—it is the need of light.

Even as the plant unalterably follows the day and the sun, even as the mollusc (to use a previous illustration) rises towards and prefers to live in the brighter regions—even so the bird, with its sensitive eye, grows melancholy in the shortened days and gathering mists of autumn.   That decline of light, which is sometimes dear to us for moral causes, is for the bird a grief, a death.   Light! more light! Let us rather die than see the day no more!   This is the true purport of its last autumnal strain, its last cry on its departure in October. I comprehended it in our friends' farewells.

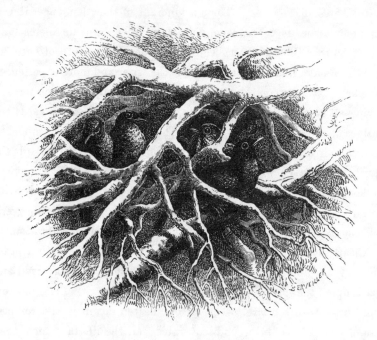

Their resolution is truly bold and courageous, when one thinks on the tremendous journey they must achieve, twice every year, over mountains, and seas, and deserts, under such diverse climates, by variable winds, through many perils, and such tragical adventures. For the light and hardy birds of flight; for the church-martin; for the keen swallow which defies the falcon; the enterprise perhaps is trivial.   But other tribes have neither their strength nor their wings; most of them are at this time heavy with abundant food; they have passed through the glowing time of love and maternity; the female has finished that grand work of nature—has given birth to, and brought up her callow brood; her mate, how he has spent his vigour in song! These two, then, have consummated life; a virtue has gone out from them; an age already separates them from the fresh energy of their spring.

Many would remain, but a goad impels them forward. The slowest are the most ardent. The French quail will traverse the Mediterranean, and cross the range of Atlas; sweeping over the Sahara, it will plunge into the kingdoms of the Negro; these, too, it will leave behind; and, finally, if it pauses at the Cape, it is because there the infinite Austral ocean commences, which promises it no nearer shelter than the icy wastes of the Pole, and the very winter which exiled it from Egypt.

What gives them confidence for such enterprises? Some may trust to their arms, the weakest to their numbers, and abandon themselves to fate. The stock-dove says: "Out of ten or a hundred thousand the assassin cannot slay more than ten, and doubtlessly I shall not be one of the victims." They seize their opportunity; the flying cloud passes at night; if the moon rise, against her silver radiance the black wings stand out clear and distinct; but they escape, confused, in her pale lustre. The valiant lark, the national bird of our ancient Gaul and of all-invincible hope, also trusts to his numbers; he sets out in the day-time, or rather, he wanders from province to province; hunted, decimated, he does not the less give utterance to his song.

But the lonely bird, which has the support neither of numbers nor of strength, what will become of him? What wilt thou do, poor solitary nightingale, which, like others of thy race, must confront this great adventure, but without assistance, without comrades? Thou, what art thou, friend? A Voice! The very power which is in thee will be thy betrayal. In thy sombre attire, thou mightst well pass unseen by blending with the tints of the discoloured woods of autumn. But see now! The leaf is still purple; it wears not the dull dead brown of the later months.

Ah, why dost thou not remain? why not imitate the timorousness of those birds which in such myriads fly no further than

Provence ?   There, sheltered behind a rock, thou shalt find, I assure thee, an Asiatic or African winter.   The gorge of Ollioules is worth all the valleys of Syria.

" No ; I must depart.   Others may tarry ; for *they* have only to gain the East.   But me, my cradle summons *me :* I must see again that glowing heaven, those luminous and sumptuous ruins where my ancestors lived and sang ; I must plant my foot once more on my earliest love, the rose of Asia ; I must bathe myself in the sunshine. *There* is the mystery of life, there quickens the flame in which my song shall be renewed ; my voice, my muse is the light."

Thus, then, he takes wing ; but I think his heart must throb when, as he approaches the Alps, their snowy peaks announce his

proximity to the terror-haunted gate on whose rocks are posted the cruel children of day and night, the vulture, the eagle—all the hooked and talon-armed robbers, athirst for the warm blood of life—the accursed species which inspire the senseless poetry of man—some, *noble* murderers, which bleed quickly and drain the flowing tide ; others, *ignoble* murderers, which choke and destroy ;—in a word, all the hideous forms of massacre and death.

I imagine to myself, then, that the poor little musician whose voice is silenced—not his *ingegno*, nor his delicate thought—having no friend to consult, will pause and anxiously reflect, before entering upon the long ambush of the pass of Savoy. He halts at the threshold, or on a friendly roof, well known to myself, or in the hallowed groves of the Charmettes,* deliberates and says : "If I pass during the day, they will all be there ; they know the season ; the eagle will pounce upon me ; I die. If I pass by night, the great horn-owl (*duc*), the common owl (*hibou*), the entire host of horrible phantoms, with eyes enlarged in the darkness, will seize me, and carry me off to their young. Alas ! what shall I do ? I must endeavour to avoid both night and day. At the gloomy hour of dawn, when the cold, raw air chills in his eyrie the great fierce beast, which knows not how to build a nest, I may fly unperceived. And even if he see me, I shall be leagues away before he can put into motion the cumbrous machinery of his frozen wings."

The calculation is judicious, but nevertheless a score of accidents may disturb it. Starting at midnight, he may encounter in the face, during his long flight across Savoy, the east wind, which engulfs and delays him, neutralizes his exertions, and fetters his pinions. Heavens! it is morning now. Those sombre giants, already clothed in October in their snowy mantles, reveal upon their vast expanse of glittering white a black spot, which moves with terrible rapidity. How gloomy are they already, these mountains, and of what evil augury, draped in the long folds of their winter shrouds ! Motionless as are their peaks, they create beneath them and around them an everlasting agitation of violent and antagonistic currents, which struggle with one another so furiously that at times they compel the bird to tarry. "If I fly in the lower air, the torrents which hurl through the shadows with their clanging floods, will snare me in their whirling vapours. And if I mount to the cold and lofty realms, which kindle with a light of their own, I give myself up to death ; the frost will seize and slacken my wings."

An effort has saved him. With head bent low, he plunges, he falls into Italy. At Susa or in the neighbourhood of Turin he builds a nest, and strengthens his pinions. He recovers himself in the depth of the

* The favourite haunt of Jean Jacques Rousseau, on the bank of Lake Leman.

gigantic Lombard *corbeille*, that great nursery of fruits and flowers where Virgil listened to his song. The land has in nowise changed ; now, as then, the Italian, an exile from his home, the sad cultivator ot another's fields,* the *durus arator*, pursues the nightingale. The useful insect-devourer is proscribed as an eater of grain. Let him cross then, if he can, the Adriatic, from isle to isle, despite the winged corsairs which keep watch on the very rocks ; he will arrive, perhaps, in the land ever consecrated to birds—in genial, hospitable, bountiful Egypt—where all are spared, nourished, blessed, and kindly welcomed.

Still happier land, if in its blind hospitality it did not also shelter the murderer. The nightingale and dove are gladly entertained, it is true, but no less so the eagle. On the terraces of sultans, on the balconies of minarets, ah, poor traveller, I see those flashing dreadful eyes which dart their gaze this way. And I see that they have already marked thee !

Do not remain here long. Thy season will not last. The destructive wind of the desert will dry up, and destroy, and sweep away thy meagre nourishment. Not a gnat will be left to sustain thy wing and thy voice. Bethink thyself of the nest which thou hast left in our woods, remember thy European loves. The sky was gloomy, but there thou madest for thyself a sky of thine own. Love was around thee ; every soul thrilled at thy voice ; the purest throbbed for thee. There shines the real sun, there beams the fairest Orient. True light is where one loves.

* This was written before the annexation of Lombardy to the new Italian kingdom.

MIGRATIONS—THE SWALLOW.

MIGRATIONS : CONTINUED.

THE SWALLOW.

UNDOUBTEDLY the swallow has seized upon our dwellings without ceremony; she lodges under our windows, under our eaves, in our chimneys. She does not hold us in the slightest fear.

It might have been said that she trusted to her unrivalled wing, had she not placed her nest and her children within our reach. The true reason why she has become the mistress of our house is, that she has taken possession not only of our house, but of our heart.

In the rural mansion where my father-in-law educated his children, he would hold his class during summer in a greenhouse in which the swallows rested without disturbing themselves about the movements of the family, quite unconstrained in their behaviour, wholly occupied with their brood, passing out at the windows and returning through the roof, chattering very loudly with one another, and still more loudly when the master would make a pretence of saying, as St. Francis said, " Sister swallows, can you not be silent ? "

Theirs is the hearth. Where the mother has built her nest, the daughter and the grand-daughter build. They return there every year ; their generations succeed to it more regularly than do our own. A family dies out or is dispersed, the mansion passes into other hands ; but the swallow constantly returns to it, and maintains its right of occupation.

It is thus that our traveller has come to be accepted as a symbol of the permanency of home. She clings to it with such fidelity, that though the house may be repaired, or partially demolished, or long disturbed by masons, it is still retaken possession of, re-occupied by these faithful birds of persevering memory.

She is the *bird of return*. And if I bestow this title upon her, it is not alone on account of her annual return, but on account of her general conduct, and the direction of her flight, so varied, yet nevertheless circular, and always returning upon itself.

She incessantly wheels and *veers*, indefatigably hovers about the same area and the same locality, describing an infinity of graceful curves, which, however varied, are never far distant from one another. Is it to pursue her prey, the gnat which dances and floats in the air ? Is it to exercise her power, her unwearying wing, without going too far from her nest ? It matters not ; this revolving flight, this incessantly returning movement, has always attracted our eyes and heart, throwing us into a reverie, into a world of thought.

We see her flight clearly, but never, or scarcely ever, her little

black face.   Who, then, art thou, thou who always concealest thyself,
who never showest me aught
but thy trenchant wings —
scythes rapid as that of Time?
But Time goes forward without
pause; thou, thou always re-
turnest.   Thou drawest close to
my side; it seems as if thou
wouldst graze me, wouldst touch
me?—So nearly dost thou caress
me, that I feel in my face the
wind, almost the whirr of thy
wings.   Is it a bird?   Is it
a spirit?   Ah, if thou art a
soul, tell me so frankly, and
reveal to me the barrier which
separates the living from the
dead.

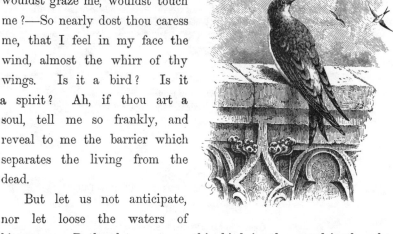

But let us not anticipate,
nor let loose the waters of
bitterness.   Rather let us trace this bird in the people's thoughts,
in the good old popular wisdom, close akin, undoubtedly, to the
wisdom of Nature.

The people have seen in her only the natural dial, the division of
the seasons, of the two great *hours of the year*.   At Easter and at
Michaelmas, at the epochs of family gatherings, of fairs and markets,
of leases and rent-paying, the black and white swallow appears, and
tells us the time.   She comes to separate and define the past and the
coming seasons.   At these epochs families and friends meet together,
but not always to find the circle complete; in the last six months
first one and then another friend have passed away.   The swallow
returns, but not for all; many have gone a very long journey, longer
than *the tour of France*.   To Germany?   No; further, further still.

Our *companions*, industrious travellers, followed the swallow's

life, except that on their return they frequently could no longer find
their nest.   Of this the pendant bird warns them in an old German
saying, wherein the narrow popular wisdom would fain retain them
round the roof-tree of home.   On this proverb, the great poet Rückert,
metamorphosing himself into a swallow, reproducing her rhythmical
and circular flight, her constant turns and returns, has founded a lyric
at which many will laugh, but more than one will weep :—

"De la jeunesse, de la jeunesse,
   Un chant me revient toujours—
Oh! que c'est loin! Oh! que c'est loin
   Tout ce qui fut autrefois ;

"Ce que chantait, ce que chantait
   Celle qui ramène le printemps,
Rasant le village de l'aile, rasant le village de l'aile,
   Est-ce bien ce qu'elle chante encore?

"'Quand je partis, quand je partis,
   Etaient pleins l'armoire et le coffre.
Quand je revins, quand je revins,
   Je ne trouvai plus que le vide.'

"O mon foyer de famille,
   Laisse-moi seulement une fois
M'asseoir à la place sacrée
   Et m'envoler dans les songes !

"Elle revient bien l'hirondelle,
   Et l'armoire vidée se remplit.
Mais le vide du cœur reste, mais reste le vide du cœur.
   Et rien ne le remplira.

"Elle rase pourtant le village,
   Elle chante comme autrefois—
'Quand je partis, quand je partis,
   Coffre, armoire, tout était plein.
Quand je revins, quand je revins
   Je ne trouvai plus que le vide.'"

Imitated:—

From childhood gay, from childhood gay,
  E'er breathes to me a strain,
How far the day, how far the day
  Which ne'er may come again!

And is her song, and is her song—
  She who brings back the spring,
The hamlet touching with her wing, the hamlet touching with her wing—
  Is it true what she doth sing?

" When I set forth, when I set forth,
  Both barn and chest were brimming o'er:
When I came back, when I came back,
  I found a piteous lack of store."

Oh, my own home, so dearly loved.
  Kind Heaven grant that I may kneel
Again upon thy sacred hearth,
  While dreams the happy past reveal!

The swallow surely will return,
  Coffer and barn will brim once more;
But blank remains the heart, empty the heart remains,
  And none may the lost restore!

The swallow skims through the hamlet,
  She sings as she sang of yore:—
" When I set out, when I set out,
  Both barn and chest were brimming o'er;
When I came back, when I came back,
  I found a piteous lack of store."

The swallow, caught in the morning, and closely examined, is seen to be a strange and ugly bird, we confess; but this fact perfectly well agrees with what is, *par excellence*, the *bird*—the being among all beings born for flight. To this object Nature has sacrificed everything; she has laughed at *form*, thinking only of *movement;* and has succeeded so well that our bird, however ugly in repose, is, when flying, the most beautiful of all.

Scythe-like wings; projecting eyes; no neck (in order to treble her strength); feet, scarcely any, or none: all is wing. These are her great general features. Add a very large beak, always open, which, in flight, snaps at its prey without stopping, closes, and again re-opens. Thus she feeds while flying; she drinks, she bathes while flying; while flying, she feeds her young.

If she does not equal in accuracy of line the thunderous swoop of the falcon, by way of compensation she is freer; she wheels, makes a hundred circles, a labyrinth of undefined figures, a maze of varied curves, which she crosses and re-crosses, *ad infinitum*. Her enemy is dazzled, lost, confused, and knows not what to do. She wearies and exhausts him; he gives up the chase, but leaves her unfatigued. She is the true queen of the air; the incomparable agility of her motions makes all space her own. Who, like her, can change in the very moment of springing, and turn abruptly? No one. The infinitely varied and capricious pursuit of a prey which is ever fluttering—of the gnat, the fly, the beetle, the thousand insects that waver to and fro and never keep in the same direction—is, undoubtedly, the best training school for flight, and renders the swallow superior to all other birds.

Nature, to attain this end, to achieve this unique wing, has adopted an extreme resolution, that of suppressing the foot. In the large church-haunting swallow, which we call the swift, the foot is reduced to a mere nothing. The wing gains in proportion; the swift, it is said, accomplishes eighty leagues in an hour. This astounding swiftness equals even that of the frigate-bird. The foot, remarkably short in the latter, is but a stump in the swift; if he rests, it is on his belly; so that he never perches. With him it is

the reverse of all other beings; movement alone affords him repose.
When he darts from the church-towers, and
commits himself to the air, the air cradles
him amorously, supports, and refreshes
him. If he would cling to any object, he
has only his own small and feeble claws.
But when he rests, he is infirm, and, as it
were, paralyzed; he feels every roughness;
the hard fatality of gravitation has resumed possession of him; the chief among
birds seems sunk to a reptile.

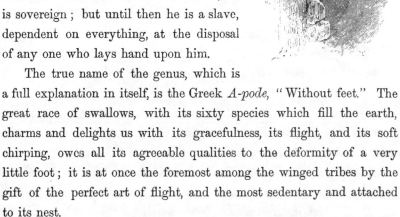

To take the range of a place is a great
difficulty for him: so, if he fixes his nest
aloft, at his departure from it he is constrained to let himself fall into his natural
element. Afloat in the air he is free, he
is sovereign; but until then he is a slave,
dependent on everything, at the disposal
of any one who lays hand upon him.

The true name of the genus, which is
a full explanation in itself, is the Greek *A-pode*, "Without feet." The
great race of swallows, with its sixty species which fill the earth,
charms and delights us with its gracefulness, its flight, and its soft
chirping, owes all its agreeable qualities to the deformity of a very
little foot; it is at once the foremost among the winged tribes by the
gift of the perfect art of flight, and the most sedentary and attached
to its nest.

Among this peculiar genus, the foot not supplying the place of
the wing, the training of the young being confined to the wing alone
and a protracted apprenticeship in flying, the brood keep the nest for a
long time, demanding the cares and developing the foresight and tenderness of the mother. The most mobile of birds is found fettered by
her affections. Her nest is not a transient nuptial bed, but a home,
a dwelling-place, the interesting theatre of a difficult education and

of mutual sacrifices.   It has possessed a loving mother, a faithful mate, — what do I say ? — rather, young sisters, which eagerly hasten to assist the mother, are themselves little mothers, and the nurses of a still younger brood.   It has developed maternal tenderness, the anxieties and mutual teaching of the young to the younger.

The finest thing is, that this sentiment of kinship expands.   In danger, every swallow is a sister ; at the cry of one, all rush to her aid ; if one be captured, all lament her, and torture their bosoms in the attempt to release her.

That these charming birds extend their sympathy to birds foreign to their own species one easily conceives.   They have less cause than any others to dread the beasts of prey, from their lightness of wing, and they are the first to warn the poultry-coops of their appearance. Hen and pigeon cower and seek an asylum as soon as they hear the swallow's signal-notes.

No; man does not err in considering the swallow the best of the winged world.

And why ?   She is the happiest, because the freest.

Free by her admirable flight.

Free by her facility of nourishment.

Free by her choice of climate.

Also, whatever attention I have paid to her language (she speaks amicably to her sisters, rather than sings), I have never heard her do aught but bless life and praise God.

Libertà ! molto e desiato bene !   I revolved these words in my heart on the great piazza of Turin, where we never wearied of watching the flight of innumerous swallows, hearing a thousand little joyous cries.   On their descent from the Alps they found numerous convenient habitations all prepared for their reception, in the apertures left by the scaffold-beams in the very walls of the palaces.   At times, and frequently in the evening, they chattered very loudly and cried shrilly, to prevent us from understanding them.   Often they darted down headlong, just skimming the ground, but rising again so quickly that one might have thought them loosened from a spring or shot from a bow.   Unlike man, who is incessantly called back to earth, they seem to gravitate above.   Never have I seen the image of a more sovereign liberty.   Their tricks, their sports, were infinite.

We travellers regarded with pleased eyes these other travellers, which bore their pilgrimage so gaily and so lightly.   The horizon, nevertheless, was heavy, and ringed by the Alps, which at that hour seemed close at hand.   The black pine-woods were already darkened and overshadowed by the evening ; the glaciers glittered again with a ghastly whiteness.   The sorrowful barrier of these grand mountains separated us from France, towards which we were soon about to travel slowly.

HARMONIES OF THE TEMPERATE ZONE.

HARMONIES OF THE TEMPERATE ZONE.

WHY do the swallow and so many other birds place their habitation so near to that of man? Why do they make themselves our friends, mingling with our labours, and lightening them by their songs? Why is that happy spectacle of alliance and harmony, which is the end of nature, presented only in the climates of our temperate zone?

For this reason, that here the two parties, man and the bird, are free from the burdensome fatalities which in the south separate them, and place them in antagonism to one another.

That which enervates man, on the contrary, excites the bird, endows him with ardent activity, inquietude, and the vehemence which finds vents in harsh cries. Under the Tropics both are in complete divergence, slaves of a despotic nature, which weighs upon them differently.

To pass from those climates to ours is to become free.

Here we dominate over the nature which *there* subjugated us. I quit willingly, and without one wistful glance, the overwhelming paradise where, like a feeble child, I languished in the arms of the great nurse who, with a too potent draught, intoxicated while thinking to suckle me.

This milder nature was made for me, is my legitimate spouse—I recognize her.   And, above all, she resembles me; like me, she is grave, she is laborious, she has the instinct of work and patience.

Her renewed seasons share among themselves her great annual day, as the workman's day alternates between toil and repose.   She gives no fruit gratuitously ; she gives what is worth all the fruits of earth—industry and activity.

With what rapture I find there to-day my image, the trace of my will, the creations of my exertions and my intelligence !   Deeply laboured by me, largely metamorphosed, she relates to me my works, and reproduces myself.   I see her as she was before she underwent this human creative work, before she was made man.

Monotonous at the first glance, and melancholy, she exhibited her forests and meadows ; but both strangely different from those which are seen elsewhere.

The meadow, the rich green carpet of England and Ireland, with its delicate soft sward constantly springing up afresh—not the rough fleece of the Asiatic steppes, not the spiny and hostile vegetation of Africa, not the bristling savagery of American savannahs, where the smallest plant is woody and harshly arborescent—the European meadow, owing to its annual and ephemeral vegetation, its lowly little flowers, and mild and gentle odours, wears a youthful aspect ; nay, more, an aspect of innocence, which harmonizes with our thoughts and refreshes our hearts.

On this first layer of humble yielding herbage, which has no pretensions to mount higher, stands out in bold contrast the strong individuality of the robust trees, so different from the confused vegetation of meridional forests.

Who can single out, beneath such a mass of lianas, orchids, and parasitical plants, the trees, themselves herbaceous, which are there, so to speak, engulphed ?   In our ancient forests of Gaul and Germany stand, strong and serious, slowly and solidly built, the elm or the oak—that forest hero, with kindly arms and heart of steel, which has conquered eight or ten centuries, and which, when felled by man and associated with his labours, endows them with the eternity of the works of nature.

As the tree, so the man. May it be given us to resemble it—to resemble that mighty but pacific oak, whose powerful absorption has concentrated every element, and made of it the grave, useful, enduring individual—the solid personality—of which all men confidently demand a support, a shelter; which stretches forth its helpful arms to the divers animal tribes, and shelters them with its foliage! With a thousand voices they gratefully enchant, by day and night, the still majesty of this aged witness of the years. The birds thank it from their hearts, and delight its paternal shades with song, love, and youth.

Indestructible vigour of the climates of the West? Why doth this oak live through a thousand years? Because it is ever young.

It is the oak which chronicles the commencement of spring. For us the emotion of the new life does not begin when all nature clothes itself in the uniform verdure of the meaner vegetation. It commences only when we see the oak, from the woody foliage of the past, which it still retains, gathering its fresh leaves; when the elm, permitting itself

to be outstripped by inferior trees, tints with a light green the severe delicacy of its airy branches, clearly defined against the sky.

Then, then, Nature speaks to all—her potent voice troubles even the soul of sages. And why not? Is she not holy? And this surprising resurrection, which has stirred life everywhere—from the hard dumb heart of the oaks, even to their lofty crest, where the bird pours out its gladness—is it not, as it were, a return of God?

I have lived in climates where the olive and the orange preserve an eternal bloom. Without ignoring the beauty of these favoured trees, and their special distinction, I could never accustom myself to the monotonous permanency of their unchangeable garb, whose verdure responded to the heaven's unchangeable sapphire.   I was ever in a state of expectancy, waiting for a renewal which never came.   The days passed by, but were always identical.   Not a leaf the less on the ground, not a cloudlet in the sky.   Mercy, I exclaimed, O ever-lasting Nature !   To the changeful heart which thou hast given me, grant a little change.   Rain, mire, storm, I accept them all ; so that from sky or earth the idea of movement may return to me—the idea of renovation ; that every year the spectacle of a new creation may refresh my heart, may restore to me the hope that my soul shall enjoy a similar resurrection, and, by the alternations of sleep, of death, or of winter, create for itself a new spring !

Man, bird, all nature, utter the same desire.   We exist through change.

To these forcible alternations of heat, cold, fog, and sun, melan-

choly and joyaunce, we owe the tempered, the powerful personality of
our West.   Rain wearies us to-day ; fine weather will come with the
morrow.   The splendours of the East, the marvels of the Tropics,
taken together, are not worth the first violet of Easter, the first song
of April, the blossom of the hawthorn, the glee of the young girl who
resumes her robes of white.

In the morning a potent voice, of singular freshness and clearness,
of keen metallic *timbre*, the voice of the mavis, rises aloft, and there
is no heart so sick or so sour as to hear it without a smile.

One spring, on my way to Lyons, among the intertangled vines
which the peasants laboured to raise up again, I heard a poor, old,
miserable, and blind woman singing, with an accent of extraordinary
gaiety, this ancient village lay :

> " Nous quittons nos grands habits,
> Pour en prendre de plus petits."

THE BIRD AS THE LABOURER OF MAN.

THE BIRD

AS THE LABOURER OF MAN.

THE "*miserly* agriculturist," is the accurate and forcible expression of Virgil. Miserly, and blind, in truth, for he proscribes the birds which destroy the insects and protect his crops.

Not a grain will he spare to the bird which, during the winter rains, hunted up the future insect, sought out the nests of the larvæ, examined them, turned over every leaf, and daily destroyed myriads of future caterpillars; but sacks of corn to the adult insects, and whole fields to the grasshoppers which the bird would have combated!

With his eyes fixed on the furrow, on the present moment, without sight or foresight; deaf to the grand harmony which no one ever interrupts with impunity, he has everywhere solicited or approved the laws which suppressed the much-needed assistant of his labour, the insect-destroying bird. And the insects have avenged the bird.   It has become necessary to recall in all haste the banished.   In the island of Bourbon, for example, a price was set on each martin's head; they disappeared, and then the grasshoppers took possession of the island, devouring, extinguishing, burning up with harsh acridity all that they did not devour.   The same thing has occurred in North America with the starling, the protector of the maize.   The sparrow even, which attacks the grain, but also defends it—the thieving, pilfering sparrow, loaded with so many insults, and stricken with so many maledictions—it has been seen that without him Hungary would perish; that he alone could wage the mighty war against the cockchafers and the myriad winged foes which reign in the low-lying lands : his banishment has been revoked, and the courageous militia hastily recalled which, if not strictly disciplined, are not the less the salvation of the country.

No long time ago, near Rouen, and in the valley of Monville, the crows had for a considerable period been proscribed.   The cockchafers, accordingly, profited to such an extent—their larvæ, multipled *ad infinitum*, pushed so far their subterranean works—that an entire meadow was pointed out to me as completely withered on the surface; every root of grass or herb was eaten up ; and all the turf, easily detached, could be rolled back on itself just as one raises a carpet.

All toil, all appeals of man to nature, supposes the intelligence of the natural order.   Such is the order, and such the law : *Life has around it and within it its enemy—most frequently as its guest—the parasite which undermines and cankers it.*

Inert and defenceless life, especially vegetable, deprived of locomotion, would succumb to it but for the stronger support of the indefatigable enemy of the parasite, the merciless pursuer, the winged conqueror of the monsters.

The war rages *without* under the Tropics, where they surge up on all sides.   *Within* in our climates, where everything is hidden, more profound, and more mysterious.

In the exuberant fecundity of the Torrid Zone, the insects, those terrible destroyers of plant-life, carry off the superfluous.   They are there a necessity.

They ravage among the ever prodigious abundance of spontaneous plants, of lost seeds, of the fruits which Nature scatters over the wastes.   Here, in the narrow field watered by the sweat of man, they garner in his place, devour his labour and its harvest ; they attack even his life.

Do not say, "Winter is on my side ; it will check the foe."   Winter does but slay the enemies which would perish of themselves.   It kills especially the ephemera, whose existence was already measured by that of the flower, or the leaf with which it was bound up.   But, before dying, the prescient atom assures the safety of its posterity; it finds for it an asylum, conceals and carefully deposits its future, the germ of its reproduction. As eggs, as larvæ, or in their own shapes, living, mature, armed, these invisible creatures sleep in the bosom of the earth, awaiting their opportunity.   Is she immovable, this earth ? In the meadows I see her undulate—the black miner, the mole, continues his labours.   At a higher elevation, in the dry grounds, stretch the subterranean granaries, where the philosophical rat, on a good pile of corn, passes the season in patience.

All this life breaks forth at spring-time. From high, from low, on the right, on the left, these predatory tribes, *échelonned* by legions which succeed one another and relieve one another each in its month, in its day—the immense, the irresistible conscription of nature—will march to the conquest of man's works. The division of labour is perfect. Each has his post marked out, and will make no mistake. Each will go straight to his tree or his plant. And such will be their tremendous numbers, that not a leaf but will have its legion.

What wilt thou do, poor man? How wilt thou multiply thyself? Hast thou wings to pursue them? Hast thou even eyes to see them? Thou mayest kill them at thy pleasure; their security is complete: kill, annihilate millions; they live by thousands of millions! Where thou triumphest by sword and fire, burning up the plant itself, thou hearest all around the light whirring of the great army of atoms, which gives no heed to thy victory, and destroys unseen.

Listen. I will give thee two counsels. Weigh them, and adopt the wiser.

The first remedy for this, if you resolve upon fighting your foe, is to poison everything. Steep your seeds in sulphate of copper; put your barley under the protection of verdigris. This the foe is unprepared for; it disconcerts him. If he touches it, he dies or sickens. You, also, it is true, are scarcely flourishing; your adventurous stratagem may help the plagues which devastate our era. Happy age! The benevolent labourer poisons at the outset; this copper-coloured corn, handed over to the baker, ferments with the sulphate; a simple and agreeable means of "raising" the light *pâte*, to which, perhaps, people would object.

No; adopt a better course than this. Take your side. Before so many enemies it is no shame to fall back. Let things go, and fold your arms. Rest, and look on. Be like that brave man who, on the eve of Waterloo, wounded and prostrate, contrived to lift himself up and scan the horizon; but he saw there Blucher, and the great cloud of the black army. Then he fell back, exclaiming, "They are too many!"

And how much more right have you to say so! You are alone against the universal conspiracy of life. You also may exclaim, "They are too many!'"

You insist. See here these fields so full of inspiring hope; see the humid pastures where I might please myself with watching the cattle lost among the thick herbage. Let us lead thither the herds!

They are expected. Without them what would become of those living clouds of insects which love nothing but blood? The blood of the ox is good; the blood of man is better. Enter; seat yourself in their midst; you will be well received, for you are their banquet. These darts, these horns, these pincers, will find an exquisite delicacy in your flesh; a sanguinary orgie will open on your body for the frantic dance of this famished host, which will not relax at least from want; you shall see more than one fall away, and die of the intoxicating fountain which he had opened with his dart. Wounded, bleeding, swollen with puffed-up sores, hope for no repose. Others will come, and again others, for ever, and without end. For if the climate is less severe than in the zones of the South, in revenge, the eternal rain—that ocean of soft warm water incessantly flooding our meadows—hatches in a hopeless fecundity those nascent and greedy lives, which are impatient to rise, to be born, and to finish their career by the destruction of superior existences.

I have seen, not in the marshes, but on the western heights, those pleasant verdurous hills, clothed with woods or meadows—I have seen the pluvial waters repose for lack of outlet; and then, when evaporated by the sun's rays, leave the earth covered with a rich and abundant animal production——slugs, snails, insects of a myriad species, all people of terrible appetite, born with sharp teeth, with formidable apparatus, and ingenious machines of destruction. Powerless against the irruption of an unexpected host which crawled, stirred, ascended, penetrated, had almost eaten up ourselves, we contended with them through the agency of some brave and voracious fowls, which never counted their enemies, and did not criticise, but swallowed them. These Breton and Vendean fowls, inspired with the genius of their country, made their campaign so much the more successfully, because each waged war in its own manner. The *black*, the *gray*, and the *egg-layer* (such were their military titles), marched together in close array, and recoiled not a step; the *dreamer* or *philosopher* preferred skirmishing by himself (*chouanner*), and accomplished much more work. A superb black cat, the companion of their solitude, studied daily the track of the field mouse and the lizard, hunted the wasp, devoured the Spanish fly, always at some distance in advance of the respectful hens.

One word more in reference to them, and one regret. Our business being finished, we prepared for our departure. But what would become of *them?* Given to a friend, they would assuredly be eaten. We deliberated long. Then, coming to a vigorous decision, according to the ancient creed of savage tribes, who believed that it was sweetest to die by the hands of those we love, and thought that by eating their heroes they themselves became heroic, we made of them, not without lamentation, a funereal banquet.

It is a truly grand spectacle to see descend—one might almost say from heaven — against this frightful swarming of the universal monster-birth which awakens in the spring, hissing, whirring, croaking, buzzing, in its huge hunger, the universal saviour, in a hundred forms and a hundred legions, differing in arms and character, but all endowed with wings, all sharing a seeming privilege of ubiquity.

To the universal presence of the insect, to its ubiquity of numbers, responds that of the bird, of his swiftness, of his wing. The great moment is that when the insect, developing itself through the heat,

meets the bird face to face; the bird multiplied in numbers; the bird which, having no milk, must feed at this very moment a numerous family with her living prey. Every year the world would be endangered if the bird could suckle, if its aliment were the work of an individual, of a stomach. But see, the noisy, restless brood, by ten, twenty, or thirty little bills, cry out for their prey; and the exigency is so great, such the maternal ardour to respond to this demand, that the desperate tomtit, unable to satisfy its score of children with three hundred caterpillars a day, will even invade the nests of other birds and pick out the brains of their young.

From our windows, which opened on the Luxemburg, we observed every winter the commencement of this useful war of the bird against the insect. We saw it in December inaugurate the year's labour. The honest and respectable household of the thrush, which one might call the leaf-lifter (*tourne-feuilles*), did their work by couples; when the sunshine followed rain, they visited the pools, and lifted the leaves one by one, with skill and conscientiousness, allowing nothing to pass which had not been attentively examined.

Thus, in the gloomiest months, when the sleep of nature so closely resembles death, the bird continued for us the spectacle of life. Even among the snow, the thrush saluted us when we arose. During our grave winter walks we were always accompanied by the wren, with his golden crest, his short, quick song, his soft and flute-like recall. The more familiar sparrows appeared on our balconies; punctual to the hour, they knew that twice a-day their meal would be ready for them, without any peril to their freedom.

For the rest, the honest labourers, on the arrival of spring, scrupled to ask our aid. As soon as their young were able to fly, they joyously brought them to our windows, as if to thank and bless us.

LABOUR—THE WOODPECKER.

LABOUR.

THE WOODPECKER.

AMONG the calumnies of which birds have been made the victims, none is more absurd than to say, as it has been said, that the woodpecker, when burrowing among the trees, selects the robust and healthy trunks, those that offer the greatest difficulties, and must increase his toil. Common sense plainly shows that the poor animal, living upon worms and insects, will seek the infirm, the rotten trees, those offering the least resistance, and promising, moreover, the most abundant prey. The persistent hostility which he wages against the destructive tribes that would corrupt the vigorous trunk, is a signal service rendered to man. The State owes him, if not the appointment, at least the honorary title, of Conservator of the Forests. But what is the fact? That for all his reward, ignorant officials have often set a price upon his head!

But the woodpecker would be no true type of the workman if he were not calumniated and persecuted. His modest guild, spread over the two worlds, serves, teaches, and edifies man. His garb varies; but the common sign by which he may be recognized is the scarlet hood with which the good artisan generally covers his head, his firm and solid skull. His special tool, which is at once pickaxe and auger, chisel and plane, is his square-fashioned bill. His nervous limbs, armed with strong black nails of a sure and firm grasp, seat him securely on his branch, where he remains for whole days, in an awkward attitude, striking always from below upwards. Except in the morning, when he bestirs himself, and stretches his limbs in every direction, like all superior workmen, who allow a few moments' preparation in order not to interrupt themselves afterwards, he digs and digs throughout a long day with singular perseverance. You may hear him still later, for he prolongs his work into the night, and thus gains some additional hours.

His constitution is well adapted for so laborious a life. His muscles, always stretched, render his flesh hard and leathery. The vesicle of the gall, in him very large, seems to indicate a bilious disposition, eager and violent in work, but otherwise by no means choleric.

Necessarily the opinions which men have pronounced on this singular being are widely different. They have judged this great worker well or ill, according as they have esteemed or despised work, according as they themselves have been more or less laborious, and have regarded a sedentary and industrious life as cursed or blessed by Heaven.

It has often been questioned whether the woodpecker was gay or melancholy, and various answers have been given—perhaps all equally good—according to species and climate. I can easily believe that Wilson and Audubon, who chiefly refer to the golden-winged woodpecker of the Carolinas, on the threshold of the Tropics, have found him very lively and restless; this woodpecker gains his livelihood without toil in a genial country, rich in insects; his curved elegant beak, less rugged than the beak of our species, seems to indicate that he works in less rebellious woods. But the woodpecker of France and Germany, compelled to pierce the bark of our ancient European oaks, possesses quite a different instrument —a hard, strong, and heavy bill. It is probable that he devotes more hours to his toil than his American congener. He is, as a labourer, bound by hard conditions, working more and earning less. In dry seasons especially, his lot is wretched; his prey flies from him, and retires to an extreme distance, in search of moisture. Therefore he invokes the rain, with constant cry: "*Plieu! Plieu!*" It is thus that the common people interpret his note; in Burgundy he is called *The Miller's Procurer;* woodpecker and miller, if the rain should not descend, would stand still and run the risk of starving.

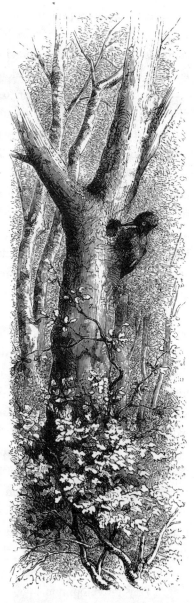

One eminent ornithologist, Toussenel, an excellent and ingenious observer, seems to me mistaken in his judgment of the woodpecker's character, when he pronounces him a lively bird. For on what grounds? On the amusing curvets in which he indulges to gain the heart of his love. But who among us, or among more serious beings, in such a case, does not do the same? He calls him also a tumbler and a clown, because at his appearance he wheeled round rapidly. For a bird whose powers of flight are very limited, it was perhaps the wisest course to adopt, especially in the presence of such an admirable shot. And this proved his good sense. A vulgar sportsman, the woodpecker, which knows the coarseness of his flesh, would have suffered to approach him. But in the presence of such a connoisseur and so keen a friend of birds, he had great cause for fear, lest he should be impaled to adorn his collection.

I beg this illustrious writer to consider also the moral habitudes and disposition which would be acquired from such continuous toil. The *papillonne* counts for nothing here, and the length of such working-days far exceeds the convenient limit of what Fourier calls agreeable labour. The woodpecker toils alone and on his own account; undoubtedly he makes no complaint; he feels that it is for his interest to work hard and to work long. Firm on his robust legs, though in a painful attitude, he remains at his post all day, and even far into the night. Is he happy? I believe so. Gay? I doubt it. Melancholy? By no means. The passionate toil which renders us so grave, compensates by driving away sorrow.

The unintelligent artisan, or the poor over-wrought slave, whose only idea of happiness lies in immobility, would not fail to see in a life of such assiduity the malediction of Fate. The artisans of the German towns assert that he is a baker, who, in the indolent ease of his counting-house, starved the poor, deceived them, sold them false weight. And now, as a punishment, he works, they say, and must work until the day of judgment, living on insects only.

A poor and unmeaning explanation! I prefer the old Italian fable: Picus, son of Time or Saturn, was an austere hero, who scorned the deceitful love and illusions of Circe. To avoid her, he took to himself wings, and flew into the forest. If he bears no longer a human figure, he has—what is better—a foreseeing and prophetic genius; he knows that which is to come, he sees that which is to be.

A very grave opinion upon the woodpecker is pronounced by the Indians of North America. These heroes discern very clearly that the woodpecker himself was a hero. They are partial to wearing the head

of one which they name "the wiry-billed woodpecker," and believe that
his ardour and courage will pass into them. A well-founded belief,
as experience has shown. The puniest heart must feel strengthened
which sees ever present before it this eloquent symbol, saying : "I
shall be like it in strength and constancy."

Only it should be noted that, if the woodpecker be a hero, he is
the peaceful hero of labour. He asks nothing more. His beak,
which might be very formidable, and his powerful spurs, are nevertheless prepared for everything else but combat. His toil so completely
absorbs him, that no competition could stimulate him to fight. It
engulfs him, requires of him all the exertion of his faculties.

Varied and complex is his work. At first the skilful forester, full
of tact and experience, tests his tree with his hammer—I mean his

beak. He listens, as the tree resounds, to what it has to say, to
what there is within it. The process of auscultation, but recently
adopted in medicine, has been the woodpecker's leading act for some
thousands of years. He interrogates, sounds, detects by his ear the
cavernous voids which the substance of the tree presents. Such a
one, sound and vigorous in appearance, which, on account of its
gigantic size, has been marked out for the shipwright's axe, the woodpecker, by his peculiar skill, condemns as worm-eaten, rotten, sure to
fail in the most fatal manner possible, to bend in construction, or
to spring a leak and so produce a wreck.

The tree thoroughly tested, the woodpecker selects it for himself,
and establishes himself upon it ; there he will exercise his art. The
trunk is hollow, therefore rotten, therefore populous ; a tribe of
insects inhabits it. You must strike at the gate of the city. The
citizens in wild tumult attempt to escape, either through the walls of
the city, or below, through the drains. Sentinels should be posted ;
but in their default the solitary besieger watches, and from moment
to moment looks behind to snap up the passing fugitives, making use,
for this purpose, of an extremely long tongue, which he darts to and
fro like a miniature serpent. The uncertainty of the sport, and the
hearty appetite which it stimulates, fill him with passion ; his glance
pierces through bark and wood ; he is present amidst the terrors and
the counsels of his enemies. Sometimes he descends very suddenly,
in alarm lest a secret issue should save the besieged.

A tree externally sound, but rotten and corrupt within, is a
terrible image for the patriot who dreams over the destinies of cities.
Rome, at the epoch when the republic began to totter, feeling itself
like to such a tree, trembled one day as a woodpecker alighted on
the tribunal in open forum, under the very hand of the prætor. The
people were profoundly moved, and revolved the gloomiest thoughts.
But the augurs, who had been summoned, arrived : if the bird escaped
with impunity, the republic would perish ; if he remained, he threatened only him who held the bird in his hand—the prætor. This
magistrate, who was Ælius Tubero, killed the bird immediately,

died soon afterwards, and the republic endured six centuries longer.

This is grand, not ridiculous. It endured through this noble appeal to the citizen's devotion. It endured through this silent response given to it by a great heart. Such actions are fertile; they make men and heroes; they prolong the life of states.

To return to our bird: this workman, this solitary, this sublime prophet does not escape the universal law. Twice a-year he grows demented, throws off his austerity, and, shall it be said, becomes ridiculous. Happy he among men who plays the fool but twice a-year!

Ridiculous?—He is not so because he loves, but because he loves comically. Gorgeously arrayed, and in his finest plumage, relieving his somewhat sombre garb by his beautiful scarlet *grecque*, he whirls round his lady-love; and his rivals do the same.

But these innocent workers, designed for the most serious labours —strangers to the arts of the fashionable world, to the graces of the humming-birds—know not in what way to manifest their duty, and present their very humble homage but by the most uncouth cur-vettings. Uncouth at least in our opinion; they are scarcely so in the eyes of the object of these attentions. They please her, and this is all that is needed. The queen's choice declared, no battle can take place. Admirable are the manners of these good and worthy workmen. The others retire aggrieved, but with delicacy cherish religiously the right of liberty.

Do the fortunate suitor and his fair one, think you, air their idle loves wandering through the forests? Not at all. They instantly begin to work. "Show me thy talents," says she, "and let me see that I have not deceived myself." What an opportunity for an artist! She inspires his genius. From a carpenter he becomes a joiner, a cabinet-maker; from a cabinet-maker, a geometer! The regularity of forms, that divine rhythm, appears to him in love.

It is exactly the renowned history of the famous blacksmith of Anvers, Quintin Matsys, who loved a painter's daughter, and who, to

win her love, became the greatest painter of Flanders in the sixteenth
century.

" Of Vulcan swart, love an Apelles made."

(D'un noir Vulcain, l'amour fit un Appelle).

Thus, one morning the woodpecker develops into the sculptor.
With severe precision, the perfect roundness which the compass might
give, he hollows out the graceful vault of a superb hemisphere.
The whole receives the polish of marble and ivory. All kinds of
hygienic and strategic precautions are not wanting. A narrow wind-
ing entry, whose slope inclines outwards that the water may not
penetrate, favours the defence; it suffices for one head and one
courageous bill to close it.

What heart could resist all these toils? Who would not accept
this artist, this laborious purveyor for domestic wants, this intrepid
defender? Who would not believe herself able to accomplish in

safety, behind the generous rampart of this devoted champion, the
delicate mystery of maternity?

So she resists no longer, and behold the pair installed! There is

wanting now but a nuptial chant (*Hymen ! O Hymeneæ !*)   It is not
the woodpecker's fault if Nature has denied to his genius the muse of
melody.   At least, in his harsh voice one cannot mistake the impassioned accents of the heart.

May they be happy !   May a young and amiable generation
spring into life, and mature under their eyes !   Birds of prey shall
not easily penetrate here.   Only grant that the serpent, the frightful
black serpent, may never visit this nest !   Oh, that the child's rough
hand may not cruelly crush its sweet hope !   And, above all, may
the ornithologist, the friend of birds, keep afar from the spot !

If persevering toil, ardent love of family, heroic defence of liberty,
could impose respect and arrest the cruel hand of man, no sportsman
would touch this noble bird.   A young naturalist, who smothered
one in order to impale it, has told me that he sickened of the brutal
struggle, and suffered a keen remorse ; it seemed to him as if he had
committed an assassination.

Wilson appears to have felt an analogous impression.   "The first
time," says he, "that I observed this bird, in North Carolina, I
wounded him slightly in the wing, and when I caught him he gave
a cry exactly like an infant's, but so loud and lamentable that my
frightened horse nearly threw me off.   I carried him to Wilmington :
in passing through the streets, the bird's prolonged cries drew to the
doors and windows a crowd of people, especially of women, filled with
alarm.   I continued my route, and, on entering the court of the
hotel, met the master of the house and a crowd of people, alarmed
at what they heard.   Judge how this alarm increased when I asked
for what was needed both by my child and myself.   The master
remained pale and stupid, and the others were dumb with astonishment.   After having amused myself at their expense for a minute
or two, I revealed my woodpecker, and a burst of universal laughter
echoed around.   I ascended with it to my chamber, where I left it
while I paid attention to my horse's wants.   I returned at the end
of an hour, and, on opening the door, heard anew the same terrible
cry, which this time appeared to originate in grief at being discovered

in his attempts to escape. He had climbed along the window almost to the ceiling, immediately above which he had begun to excavate. The bed was covered with large pieces of plaster, the laths of the ceiling were exposed for an area of nearly fifteen square inches, and a hole through which you could pass your thumb was already formed in the skylight; so that, in the space of another hour, he would certainly have succeeded in effecting an opening. I fastened round his neck a cord, which I attached to the table, and left him— I wanted to preserve him alive—while I went in search of food. On returning, I could hear that he had resumed his labours, and on my entrance saw that he had nearly destroyed the table to which he had been fastened, and against which he had directed all his wrath. When I wished to take a sketch, he cut me several times with his beak, and displayed so noble and so indomitable a courage that I was tempted to restore him to his native forests. He lived with me nearly three days, refusing all food, and I was present at his death with sincere regret."

THE SONG.

THE SONG.

EVERY one, I think, must have remarked that
birds kept in a cage in a drawing-room never fail, if
visitors arrive and the conversation grows animated,
to take a part in it, after their fashion, by chattering
or singing.

It is their universal instinct, even in a condition
of freedom. They are the echoes both of God and of
man. They associate themselves with all sounds and
voices, add their own poesy, their wild and simple
rhythms. By analogy and by contrast, they augment
and complete the grand effects of nature. To the
hoarse beating of the waves the sea-bird opposes his shrill strident
notes; with the monotonous murmuring of the agitated trees the turtle-
dove and a hundred birds blend a soft sad cadence; to the awakening

of the fields, the gaiety of the country, the lark responds with his song, and bears aloft to heaven the joys of earth.

Thus, then, everywhere, above the vast instrumental concert of nature, above her deep sighs, above the sonorous waves which escape from the divine organ, a vocal music springs and detaches itself— that of the bird, almost always in vivid notes, which strike sharply on this solemn base with the ardent strokes of a bow.

Winged voices, voices of fire, angel voices, emanations of an intense life superior to ours, of a fugitive and mobile existence, which inspires the traveller doomed to a well-beaten track with the serenest thoughts and brightest dream of liberty !

Just as vegetable life renews itself in spring by the return of the leaves, is animal life renewed, rejuvenified by the return of the birds, by their loves, and by their strains.   There is nothing like it in the southern hemisphere, a youthful world in an inferior condition, which, still in travail, aspires to find a voice.   That supreme flower of life and the soul, Song, is not yet given to it.

The beautiful, the sublime phenomenon of this higher aspect of the world occurs at the moment that Nature commences her voiceless concert of leaves and blossoms, her melodies of March and April, her symphony of May, and we all vibrate to the glorious harmony ; men and birds take up the strain.   At that moment the smallest become poets, often sublime songsters.   They sing for their companions whose love they wish to gain.   They sing for those who hearken to them, and many there are who accomplish incredible efforts of emulation. Man also responds to the bird.   The song of the one inspires the other with song.   Harmony unknown in tropic climes!   The dazzling colours which there replace this concord of sweet sounds do not create such a mutual bond.   In a robe of sparkling gems, the bird is not less alone.

Far different from this favoured, dazzling, glittering being are the birds of our colder countries, humble in attire, rich in heart, but almost paupers.   Few, very few of them, seek the handsome gardens, the aristocratic avenues, the shade of great parks.   They all live with the peasant. God has distributed them everywhere. Woods and thickets, clearings, fields, vineyards, humid meadows, reedy pools, mountain forests, even the peaks snow-crowned—he has allotted each winged tribe to its particular region—has deprived no country, no locality, of this harmony, so that man can wander nowhere, can neither ascend so high, nor descend so low, but that he will be greeted with a chorus of joy and consolation.

Day scarcely begins, scarcely does the stable-bell ring out for the herds, but the wagtail appears to conduct, and frisk and hover around them. She mingles with the cattle, and familiarly accompanies the hind. She knows that she is loved both by man and the beasts, which she defends against insects. She boldly plants herself on the head of the cow, on the back of the sheep. By day she never quits them; she leads them homeward faithfully at evening.

The water-wagtail, equally punctual, is at her post; she flutters round the washerwomen; she hops on her long legs into the water, and asks for crumbs; by a strange instinct of mimicry she raises and dips her tail, as if to imitate the motion of beating the linen, to do her work also and earn her pay.

The bird of the fields before all others, the labourer's bird, is the lark, his constant companion, which he encounters everywhere in his painful furrow, ready to encourage, to sustain him, to sing to him of

hope. *Espoir*, hope, is the old device of us Gauls; and for this reason
we have adopted as our national bird that humble minstrel, so poorly
clad, but so rich in heart and song.

Nature seems to have treated the lark with harshness.   Owing to
the arrangement of her claws, she
cannot perch on the trees. She
rests on the ground, close to the
poor hare, and with no other
shelter than the furrow.   How
precarious, how riskful a life, at
the time of incubation !   What
cares must be hers, what inqui-

etudes ! Scarcely a tuft of grass conceals the mother's fond treasure
from the dog, the hawk, or the falcon.   She hatches her eggs in haste ;
with haste she trains the trembling brood.   Who would not believe
that the ill-fated bird must share the melancholy of her sad neighbour,
the hare ?

This animal is sad, and fear consumes her.

"Cet animal est triste et la crainte le ronge."

LA FONTAINE.

But the contrary has taken place by an unexpected marvel of gaiety and easy forgetfulness, of lightsome indifference and truly French carelessness; the national bird is scarcely out of peril before she recovers all her serenity, her song, her indomitable glee. Another wonder : her perils, her precarious existence, her cruel trials, do not harden her heart; she remains good as well as gay, sociable and trustful, presenting a model (rare enough among birds) of paternal love ; the lark, like the swallow, will, in case of need, nourish her sisters.

Two things sustain and animate her : love and light. She makes love for half the year. Twice, nay, thrice, she assumes the dangerous happiness of maternity, the incessant travail of a hazardous education. And when love fails, light remains and re-inspires her. The smallest gleam suffices to restore her song.

She is the daughter of day. As soon as it dawns, when the horizon reddens and the sun breaks forth, she springs from her furrow like an arrow, and bears to heaven's gate her hymn of joy. Hallowed poetry, fresh as the dawn, pure and gleeful as a childish heart ! That powerful and sonorous voice is the reapers' signal. "We must start," says the father; "do you not hear the lark ?" She follows them, and bids them have courage ; in the hot sunny hours invites them to slumber, and drives away the insects. Upon the bent head of the young girl half awakened she pours her floods of harmony.

"No throat," says Toussenel, "can contend with that of the lark in richness and variety of song, compass and *velvetiness* of *timbre*, duration and range of sound, suppleness and indefatigability of the vocal chords. The lark sings for a whole hour without half a second's pause, rising vertically in the air to the height of a thousand yards, and stretching from side to side in the realm of clouds to gain a yet loftier elevation, without losing one of its notes in this immense flight.

"What nightingale could do as much ?"

This hymn of light is a benefit bestowed on the world, and you will meet with it in every country which the sun illuminates. There are as many different species of larks as there are different countries : wood-larks, field-larks, larks of the thickets, of the marshes, the larks of the Crau de Provence, larks of the chalky soil of Champagne, larks of the northern lands in both hemispheres; you will find them, moreover, in the salt steppes, in the plains of Tartary withered by the north wind. Preserving reclamation of kindly nature ; tender consolations of the love of God !

But autumn has arrived. While the lark gathers behind the plough the harvest of insects, the guests of the northern countries come to visit us : the thrush, punctual to our vintage-time ; and, haughty under his crown, the wren, the imperceptible " King of the North." From Norway, at the season of fogs, he comes, and, under a gigantic fir-tree, the little magician sings his mysterious song, until the extreme cold constrains him to descend, to mingle, and make himself popular among the little troglodytes which dwell with us, and charm our cottages by their limpid notes.

The season grows rough ; all the birds draw nearer man. The honest bullfinches, fond and faithful couples, come, with a short melancholy chirp, to solicit help. The winter-warbler also quits his bushes ; timid as he is, he grows sufficiently bold towards evening to raise outside our doors his trembling voice with its monotonous, plaintive accents.

" When, in the first mists of October, shortly before winter, the poor proletarian seeks in the forest his pitiful provision of dead wood, a small bird approaches him, attracted by the noise of his axe ; he hovers around him, and taxes his wits to amuse him by singing in a very low voice his softest lays. It is the robin redbreast, which a charitable fairy has despatched to tell the solitary labourer that there is still some one in nature interested in him.

" When the woodcutter has collected the brands of the preceding day, reduced to cinders; when the chips and the dry branches crackle in the flames, the robin hastens singing to enjoy his share of the warmth, and to participate in the woodcutter's happiness.

" When Nature retires to slumber, and folds herself in her mantle of snow ; when one hears no other voices than those of the birds of the North, which define in the air their rapid triangles, or that of the north wind, which roars and engulfs itself in the thatched roof of the cottages, a tiny flute-like song, modulated in softest notes, protests still, in the name of creative work, against the universal weakness, lamentation, and lethargy."

Open your windows, for pity's sake, and give him a few crumbs,

a handful of grain.   If he sees friendly faces, he will enter the room ;
he is not insensible to warmth ; cheered by this brief breath of
summer, the poor little one returns much stronger into the
winter.

Toussenel is justly indignant that no poet has sung of the robin.*
But the bird himself is his own bard ; and if one could transcribe his
little song, it would express completely the humble poesy of his life.
The one which I have by my side, and which flies about my study,
for lack of listeners of his own species, perches before the glass, and,
without disturbing me, in a whispering voice utters his thoughts to
the ideal robin which he fancies he sees before him.   And here is
their meaning, so far as a woman's hand has succeeded in preserving it :—

" Je suis le compagnon
     Du pauvre bûcheron.

" Je le suis en automne,
     Au vent des premiers froids,
     Et c'est moi qui lui donne
     Le dernier chant des bois.

" Il est triste, et je chante
     Sous mon deuil mêlé d'or.
     Dans la brume pesante
     Je vois l'azur encor.

" Que ce chant te relève
     Et te garde l'espoir !
     Qu'il te berce d'un rêve,
     Et te ramène au soir !

" Mais quand vient la gelée,
     Je frappe à ton carreau.

* It is unnecessary to remind the reader that this is true only of *French* poets.—
Translator.

Il n'est plus de feuillée,
Prends pitié de l'oiseau !

" C'est ton ami d'automne
    Qui revient près de toi.
    Le ciel, tout m'abandonne—
    Bûcheron, ouvre-moi !

" Qu'en ce temps de disette,
    Le petit voyageur,
    Régalé d'une miette,
    S'endorme à ta chaleur !

" Je suis le compagnon
    Du pauvre bûcheron."

Imitated :—

I am the companion
Of the poor woodcutter.

I follow him in autumn,
When the first chill breezes plain ;
And I it is who warble
The woodlands' last sweet strain.

He is sad, and then I sing
Under my gilded shroud,
And I see the gleam of azure
Glint through the gathering cloud.

Oh, may the song inspiring
Revive Hope's flame again,
And at even guide thee homeward
By the magic of its strain !

But when the streams are frozen,
I tap at thy window-pane—
Oh, on the bird take pity,
Not a leaf, not a herb remain !

It is thy autumn comrade
Who makes appeal to thee;
By heaven, by all forsaken,
Woodman, oh, pity me!

Yes, in these days of famine
The little pilgrim keep;
On dainty crumbs regale him,
By the fireside let him sleep!

For I am the companion
Of the poor woodcutter!

THE NEST.

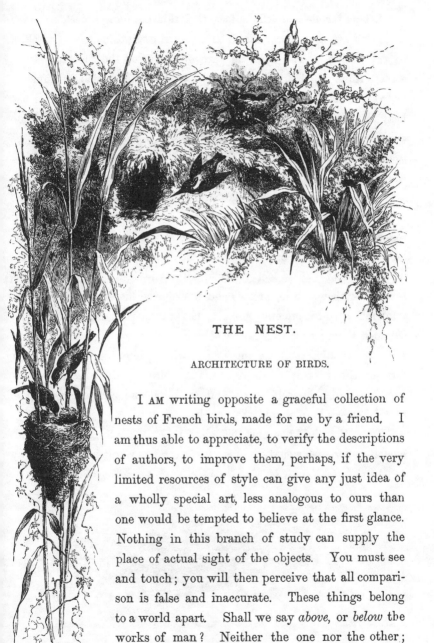

THE NEST.

ARCHITECTURE OF BIRDS.

I AM writing opposite a graceful collection of nests of French birds, made for me by a friend. I am thus able to appreciate, to verify the descriptions of authors, to improve them, perhaps, if the very limited resources of style can give any just idea of a wholly special art, less analogous to ours than one would be tempted to believe at the first glance. Nothing in this branch of study can supply the place of actual sight of the objects. You must see and touch; you will then perceive that all comparison is false and inaccurate. These things belong to a world apart. Shall we say *above*, or *below* the works of man? Neither the one nor the other; but essentially different, and whose supposed similarities (or relations) are only external.

Let us recollect, at the outset, that this charming object, so much more delicate than words can describe, owes everything to art, to skill, to calculation.   The materials are generally of the rudest, and not always those which the artist would have preferred.   The instruments are very defective.   The bird has neither the squirrel's hand nor the beaver's tooth.   Having only his bill and his foot (which by no means serves the purpose of a hand), it seems that the nest should be to him an insoluble problem.   The specimens now before my eyes are for the most part composed of a tissue or covering of mosses, small flexible branches, or long vegetable filaments ; but it is less a *weaving* than a *condensation ;* a felting of materials, blended, beaten, and welded together with much exertion and perseverance ; an act of great labour and energetic operation, for which the bill and the claw would be insufficient.   The tool really used is the bird's own body—his breast—with which he presses and kneads the materials until he has rendered them completely pliable, has thoroughly mixed them, and subdued them to the general work.

And within, too, the implement which determines the circular form of the nest is no other than the bird's body.   It is by constantly turning himself about, and ramming the wall on every side, that he succeeds in shaping the circle.

Thus, then, his house is his very person, his form, and his immediate effort—I would say, his suffering.   The result is obtained only

by a constantly repeated pressure of his breast.   There is not one of these blades of grass but which, to take and retain the form of a curve, has been a thousand and a thousand times pressed against his bosom, his heart, certainly with much disturbance of the respiration, perhaps with much palpitation.

It is quite otherwise with the habitat of the quadruped. He comes into the world clothed; what need has he of a nest? Thus, then, those animals which build or burrow labour for themselves rather than for their young. A skilful miner is the mountain rat, in his oblique tunnel, which saves him from the winter gale. The squirrel, with hand adroit, raises the pretty turret which defends him from the rain. The great engineer of the lakes, the beaver, foreseeing the gathering of the waters, builds up several stages to which he may ascend at pleasure; but all this is done for the individual. The bird builds for her family. Carelessly did she live in her bright leafy bower, exposed to every enemy; but the moment she was no longer alone, the hoped for and anticipated maternity made her an artist. The nest is a creation of love.

Thus, the work is imprinted with a force of extraordinary will, of a passion singularly persevering. You see in it especially this fact, that it is not, like our works, prepared from a model, which settles the plan, conducts and regulates the labour. Here the conception is so thoroughly *in* the artist, the idea so clearly defined, that, without frame or carcase, without preliminary support, the aerial ship is built up piece by piece, and not a hitch disturbs the *ensemble*. All adjusts itself exactly, symmetrically, in perfect harmony; a thing infinitely difficult in such a de-

ficiency of tools, and in this rude effort of concentration and kneading
by the mere pressure of the breast.   The mother does not trust to
the male bird for all this; but she employs him as her purveyor.
He goes in quest of the materials—grasses, mosses, roots, or branches.
But when the ship is built, when the interior has to be arranged—
the couch, the household furniture—the matter becomes more difficult.
Care must be taken that the former be fit to receive an egg peculiarly
sensitive to cold, every chilled point of which means for the little
one a dead limb.   That little one will be born naked.   Its stomach,
closely folded to the mother's, will not fear the cold; but the back,
still bare, will only be warmed by the bed; the mother's
precaution and anxiety are, therefore, not easily satisfied.
The husband brings her some horse-hair, but it is too
hard; it will only serve as an under-stratum, a sort of
elastic mattress.   He brings hemp, but that is too
cold; only the silk or silky fibre of certain
plants, wool or cotton, are admissible; or better
still, her own feathers, her own down, which
she plucks away, and deposits under the nursling.
It is interesting to watch the male bird's skilful and furtive search for materials; he is ap-
prehensive lest you should learn, by watching
him with your eyes, the track to his nest.
Frequently, if you look at him, he will take a
different road, to deceive you.   A hundred
ingenious little thefts respond to the mother's
desire.   He will follow the sheep
to collect a little wool.   From the
poultry-yard he will gather the drop-
ped feathers of the mother hen.   If
the farmer's wife quit for a
moment her seat in the porch,
and leave behind her distaff
or ball of thread, he

will spy his opportunity, and go off the richer for a thread or two.

Collections of nests are very recent, not numerous, and, as yet, not rich. In that of Rouen, however, which is remarkable for its arrangement ; in that of Paris, where many very curious specimens may be examined; you can distinguish already the different industries which create this master-piece of the nest. What is the chronology, the gradual growth of it ? Not from one art to another (not from masonry to weaving, for example) ; but in each separate art, the birds which abandon themselves to it are more or less successful, according to the intelligence of the species, the abundance of material, or the exigency of climate.

Among the burrowing birds, the booby, and the penguin, whose young, as soon as born, spring into the sea, content themselves with hollowing out a rude hole. But the bee-eater, the sea-swallow, which must educate their young, excavate under the ground a dwelling which is admirably proportioned, and not without some geometrical design. They furnish it, moreover, and strew it with soft yielding substances on which the fledgling will be less sensitive to the hardness or freshness of the humid soil.

Among the building-birds, the flamingo, which raises a pyramid of mud to isolate her eggs from the inundated earth, and, while standing erect, hatches them under her long legs, is contented with a rude, rough work. It is, moreover, a stratagem. The true mason is the swallow, which suspends her house to ours.

The marvel of its kind is, perhaps, the wonderful carpentry which the thrush executes. The nest, very much exposed under the moist shelter of the vines, is made externally of moss, and amid the surrounding verdure escapes the eye; but look within: it is an admirable cupola, neat, polished, shining, and not inferior to glass. You may see yourself in it as in a mirror.

The rustic art, appropriate to the forests, of timber-work, joining, wood-carving, is attempted on the lowest scale by the toucan, whose bill, though enormous, is weak and thin: he attacks only worm-eaten trees. The woodpecker, better armed, as we have seen, accomplishes more: he is a true carpenter; until love inspires him, and he becomes a sculptor.

Infinite in varieties and species is the guild of basket-makers and weavers. To note the starting-point, the advance, and the climax of an industry so varied, would be a prolonged labour.

The shore birds plait, to begin with, but very unskilfully. Why should they do better? So warmly clothed by nature with an unctuous and almost impermeable coat of plumage, they have little need to allow for the elements. Their great art is the chase; always lank, and insufficiently fed, the piscivora are controlled by the wants of a craving stomach.

The very elementary weaving of the herons and storks is already outstripped, though to no great extent, by the basket-makers of the woods, the jay, the mocking-bird, the bullfinch. Their more numerous brood impose on them more arduous toil. They lay down rude enough foundations, but thereupon plant a basket of more or less elegant design, a web of roots and dry twigs strongly woven together. The cistole delicately interlaces three reeds or canes, whose leaves, mingled with the web, form a safe and mobile base, undulating as the bird rocks. The tomtit suspends her purse-like cradle to a bough, and trusts to the wind to nurse her progeny.

The canary, the goldfinch, the chaffinch, are skilful *felters*. The latter, restless and suspicious, attaches to the finished nest, with much skill and address, a quantity of white lichens, so that the spotted appearance of the whole completely misleads the seeker, and induces him to take this charming and cunningly disguised nest for an accident of vegetation, a fortuitous and natural object.

Glueing and felting play an important part in the work of the weavers. It would be a mistake to separate these arts too widely. The humming-bird consolidates its little house with the gum of trees. Most birds employ saliva. Some—a strange thing, and a subtle invention of love!—resort to difficult processes for which their organs are ill adapted. An American starling contrives to sew the leaves with its bill, and does so very adroitly.

A few skilful weavers, not satisfied with the bill, bring into play their feet. The chain prepared, they fix it with their feet, while the beak inserts the weft. They become genuine weavers.

In fine, skill never fails them. It is very astonishing, but implements *are* wanting. They are strangely ill-adapted for the work. Most insects, in comparison, are wonderfully furnished with arms and utensils. But these are true workmen, are born workmen. The bird is so but for a time, through the inspiration of love.

THE COMMUNITIES OF BIRDS.

THE COMMUNITIES OF BIRDS.

ESSAYS AT A REPUBLIC.

THE more I reflect upon it, the more clearly I perceive that the bird, unlike the insect, is not an industrial animal. He is the poet of nature, the most independent of created beings, with a sublime, an adventurous, but on the whole an ill-protected existence.

Let us penetrate into the wild American forests, and examine the means of safety which these isolated beings invent or possess. Let us compare the bird's resources, the efforts of his genius, with the inventions of his neighbour, man, who inhabits the same localities. The difference does honour to the bird; human invention is always acting on the offensive. While the Indian has fashioned a club and a tomahawk, the bird has built only a nest.

For decency, warmth, and elegant gracefulness, the nest is in every respect superior to the Indian's wigwam or the Negro's hut, which frequently, in Africa, is nothing but a baobab hollowed by time.

The negro has not yet invented the door; his hut remains open. Against the nocturnal forays of wild beasts, he protects the entrance with thorns.

Nor does the bird know how to close his nest. What shall be its defence? A great and terrible question.

He makes the entry narrow and tortuous. If he selects a natural nest, as the wryneck does, in the hollow of a tree, he contracts the opening by skilful masonry. Many, like the pine-pine, build a double nest in two apartments: the mother sits in the alcove; in the vestibule watches the father, an attentive sentinel, to repulse invasion.

What enemies has he to fear! Serpents, men or apes, squirrels! And what do I say? The birds themselves! This people, too, has its robbers. His neighbours sometimes assist a feeble bird to recover his property, to expel by force the unjust usurper. Naturalists assure us that the rooks (a kind of crow) carry further the spirit of justice. They do not pardon a young couple who, to complete their establishment the sooner, rob the materials—" the movables "—of another nest.

They assemble in a troop of eight or ten to rend in fragments the nest of the criminals, and completely destroy that house of theft. And punished thieves are driven afar, and forced to begin all over again.

Is there not here an idea of property, and of the sacred rights of labour?

Where shall they find securities, and how assure a commencement of public order? It is curious to know in what way the birds have resolved the question.

Two solutions presented themselves. The first was that of *association*—the organization of a government which should concentrate force, and by the reunion of the weak form a defensive power. The second (but miraculous? impossible? imaginative?) would have been the realization of the *aerial city* of Aristophanes,—the construction of a dwelling-place guarded by its lightness from the unwieldy brigands of the air, and inaccessible to the approaches of the brigands of the earth —the hunter, the serpent.

These two things—the one difficult, the other apparently impossible—the bird has realized.

At first, association and government. Monarchy is the inferior venture. Just as the apes have a king to conduct each band, several species of birds, especially in dangerous emergencies, appear to follow a chief.

The ant-eaters have a king; so have the birds of paradise. The tyrant, an intrepid little bird of extraordinary audacity, affords his protection to some larger species, which follow and confide in him. It is asserted that the noble hawk, repressing its instincts of prey for certain species, allows the trembling families which trust in his generosity to nestle under and around him.

But the safest fellowship is that between equals. The ostrich, the penguin, a crowd of species, unite for this purpose. Several kinds, associating for the purpose of travel, form, at the moment of emigration, into temporary republics. We know the good understanding, the republican gravity, the perfect tactics of the storks and cranes. Others, smaller in size or less completely armed—in climates, moreover, where nature, cruelly prolific, engenders without pause their formidable foes— place their abodes close together, but do not mingle them, and under a common roof, living in separate partitions, form veritable hives.

The description given by Paterson appeared fabulous ; but it has been confirmed by Levaillant, who frequently encountered in Africa, studied, and investigated the strange community. The engraving given in the "Architecture of Birds" enables the reader more readily to comprehend his narration. It is the image of an immense umbrella planted on a tree, and shading under its common roof more than three hundred habitations. " I caused it to be brought to me," says Levaillant, "by several men, who set it on a vehicle. I cut it with an axe, and saw that it was in the main a mass of Booschmannie grass, without any mixture, but so strongly woven together that it was impossible for the rain to penetrate. This is only the framework of the edifice ; each bird constructs for himself a separate nest under the common pavilion. The nests occupy only the reverse of the roof ; the upper part remains empty, without, however, being useless ; for, raised more than the remainder of the pile, it gives to the whole a sufficient inclination, and thus preserves each little habitation. In two words, let the reader figure to himself a great oblique and irregular roof, whose edge in the interior is garnished with nests ranged close to one another, and he will have an exact idea of these singular edifices.

"Each nest is three or four inches in diameter, which is sufficiently large for the bird ; but as they are in close contact around the roof, they appear to the eye to form but a single edifice, and are separated only by a small opening which serves as an entry to the nest; and one entrance frequently is common to three nests, one of which is placed at the bottom, and the others on each side. It has 320 cells, and will hold 640 inhabitants, if each contains a couple, which may be doubted. Every time, however, that I have aimed at a swarm, I have killed the same number of males and females."

A laudable example, and worthy of imitation! I wish I could but believe that the fraternity of those poor little ones was a sufficient protection. Their number and their noise may sometimes alarm the enemy, disturb the monster, make him take another direction. But if he should persist; if, strong in his scaly skin, the boa, deaf to their cries, mounts to the attack, invades the city at the time when the fledglings have as yet no wings for flight, their numbers then can but multiply the victims.

There remains the idea of Aristophanes, the *aerial city*—to isolate it from earth and water, and build in the air.

This is a stroke of genius. And to carry it out is needed the miracle of the two foremost powers in the world—love and fear.

Of the most vivid fear; of that which freezes your blood : if, peering through a hole in a tree, the black flat head of a cold reptile rises and hisses in your face, though you are a man, and a brave man, you tremble.

How much more must the little, feeble, disarmed creature, surprised in its nest, and unable to make use of its wings—how much more must it tremble, and sink panic-stricken !

The invention of the aerial city took place in the land of serpents.

Africa, the realm of monsters, in its horrible arid wastes, sees them cover the earth. Asia, on the burning shore of Bombay, in her forests where the mud ferments, makes them swarm, and fatten, and swell with venom. In the Moluccas they are innumerable.

Thence came the inspiration of the *Loxia pensilis* (the grosbeak of the Philippines). Such is the name of the great artist.

He chooses a bamboo growing close to the water. To the branches of this tree he delicately suspends some vegetable fibres. He knows beforehand the weight of the nest, and never errs. To the threads he attaches, one by one (not supporting himself on anything, but working in the air) some sufficiently strong grasses. The task is long and fatiguing; it presupposes an infinite amount of patient courage.

The vestibule alone is nothing less than a cylinder of twelve to fifteen inches, which hangs over the water, the opening being below, so that one enters it ascending. The upper extremity may be compared to a gourd or an inflated bag, like a chemist's retort. Sometimes five or six hundred nests of this kind hang to a single tree.

Such is my city of the air; not a dream and a phantasy, like that of Aristophanes, but actual, realized, and answering the three conditions : security both on the side of land and water, and inaccessibility to the robbers of the air through its narrow openings, where one can enter only by ascending with great difficulty.

Now, that which was said to Columbus when he defied his guests to make an egg stand upright, you perhaps will say to the ingenious bird in reference to his suspended city. You will observe, " It was very simple." To which the bird will reply, like Columbus, " Why did you not discover it ? "

EDUCATION.

EDUCATION.

BEHOLD, then, the nest made, and protected by every prudential means which the mother can devise. She rests upon her perfected work, and dreams of the new guest which it shall contain to-morrow.

At this hallowed moment, ought not we, too, to reflect and ask ourselves what it is this mother's bosom contains?

A soul? Shall we dare to say that this ingenious architect, this tender mother, has *a soul?*

Many persons, nevertheless, full of sense and sympathy, will denounce, will reject this very natural idea as a scandalous hypothesis.

Their heart would incline them towards it; their mind leads them to repel it; their mind, or at least their education; the idea which, from an early age, has been impressed upon them.

Beasts are only machines, mechanical automata; or if we think we can detect in them some glimmering rays of sensibility and reason, those are solely the effect of *instinct*.   But what is instinct? A sixth sense—I know not what—which is undefinable, which has been implanted in them, not acquired by themselves—a blind force which acts, constructs, and makes a thousand ingenious things, without their being conscious of them, without their personal activity counting for aught.

If it is so, this instinct would be invariable, and its works immovably regular, which neither time nor circumstances would ever change.

Indifferent minds—distracted, busy about other matters—which have no time for observation, accept this statement upon parole. Why not?   At the first glance certain actions and also certain works of animals appear *almost* regular.   To come to a different conclusion, more attention, perhaps, is needed, more time and study, than the question is fairly worth.

Let us adjourn the dispute, and see the object itself.   Let us take the humblest example, an individual example; let us appeal to our eyes, our own observation, such as each one of us can make with the most vulgar of the senses.

Perhaps the reader will permit me here to introduce, in all honesty and simpleness, the journal of my canary, Jonquille, as it was written hour by hour from the birth of her first child; a journal of remarkable exactness, and, in short, an authentic register of birth.

" It must be stated, at the outset, that Jonquille was born in a cage, and had not seen how nests were made.   As soon as I saw her disturbed, and became aware of her approaching maternity, I frequently opened her door, and allowed her freedom to collect in the room the materials of the bed the little one would stand in need of.   She gathered them up, indeed, but without knowing how to employ them.   She put them together, and stored them in a corner of her cage.   It was very evident that the art of construction was not innate in her, that (exactly like man) the bird does not know until it has learned.

"I gave her the nest ready made, at least the little basket which forms the framework and walls of the structure. Then she made the mattress, and felted the interior coating, but in a very indifferent manner. Afterwards she sat on her egg for sixteen days with a perseverance, a fervour, a maternal devotion which were astonishing, scarcely rising for a few minutes in the day from her fatiguing position, and only when the male was ready to take her place.

"At noon on the sixteenth day the shell was broken in two, and we saw, struggling in the nest, a pair of little wings without feathers, a couple of tiny feet, a something which struggled to rid itself entirely of its envelopment. The body was one large stomach, round as a ball. The mother, with great eyes, outstretched neck, and fluttering wings, from the edge of the basket looked at her child, and looked at me also, as if to say : ' Do not come near !'

"Except some long down on the wings and head, it was completely naked.

"On this first day she gave it only some drink. It opened, however, already a bill of good proportions.

"From time to time, that it might breathe the more easily, she moved a little, then replaced it under her wing, and rubbed it gently.

"The second day it ate but a very light beakful of chickweed, well prepared, brought in the first place by the father, received by the mother, and transmitted by her with short, quick chirps. In all probability this was given rather for medicinal purposes than as food.

"So long as the nursling has all it requires, the mother permits the male bird to fly to and fro, to go and come, to attend to his occupations. But as soon as it asks for more, the mother, with her sweetest voice, summons the purveyor, who fills his beak, arrives in all haste, and transmits to her the food.

"The fifth day the eyes are less prominent ; on the sixth, in the morning, feathers stretch along the wings, and the back grows darker ; on the eighth it opens its eyes when called, and begins to stutter :

the father ventures to nourish it. The mother takes some
relaxation, and frequently absents herself. She often perches
on the rim of the nest, and lovingly contemplates her offspring. But the latter stirs, feels the need of movement. Poor
mother! in a little while it will escape thee.

"In this first education of the still passive and elementary life,
as in the second (and active, that of flight), of which I have already
spoken, one fact, evident and clearly discernible at every moment,
was, that everything was proportioned with infinite prudence
to the condition least foreseen, a condition essentially variable, the
nursling's individual strength; the quantity, quality, and mode of
preparation of the food, the cares of warmth, friction, cleanliness,
were all ordered with a skill and an attention to detail, modified
according to circumstance, such as the most delicate and provident
woman could hardly have surpassed.

"When I saw her heart throbbing violently, and her eye kindling
as she gazed on her precious treasure, I exclaimed: 'Could I do
otherwise near the cradle of my son?'"

Ah, if she be a machine, what am I myself? and who will then
prove that I am a person? If she has not a soul, who will answer
to me for the human soul? To what thereafter shall we trust? And
is not all this world a dream, a phantasmagoria, if, in the most

individual actions, actions the most plainly reasoned over and calculated upon, I am to conclude there is nothing but a lack of reason, a
mechanism, an "automatism," a species of pendulum which sports
with life and thought?

Note that our observations were made on a captive, who worked
in fatal and predetermined conditions of dwelling-place, nourishment,
&c. But how, if her action had been more evidently chosen, willed,
and meditated; if all this had transpired in the freedom of the forests,
or she had had cause to disquiet herself about many other circumstances which captivity enabled her to ignore? I am thinking
especially of the anxiety for security, which, for the bird in savage
life, is the foremost of all cares, and which more than anything else
exercises and develops her free genius.

This first initiation into life, of which I have just given an
example, is followed by what I shall call the *professional education;*
every bird has a vocation.

This education is more or less arduous, according to the medium
and the circumstances in which each species is placed. That of
fishing, for instance, is simple enough for the penguin, which, in her

clumsiness, finds it difficult to conduct her brood to the sea; its great
nurse attends the little one, and offers it the food all ready; it

has but to open its bill.   With the duck, this education or training
is more complex.   I observed one summer, on a lake in Normandy,
a duck, followed by her brood, giving them their first lesson.   The
nurslings, riotous and greedy, asked but for food.   The mother, yielding to their cries, plunged to the bottom of the water, reappearing
with some small worm or little fish, which she distributed impartially,
never giving twice in succession to the same duckling!

In this picture the most touching figure was the mother, whose
stomach undoubtedly was also craving, but who retained nothing for
herself, and seemed happy in the sacrifice.   Her visible desire was to
accustom her family to do as she did, to dive under the water intrepidly to seize their prey.   With a voice almost gentle, she implored
this action of courageous confidence.   I had the happiness of seeing
the little ones plunge in, one after another, to the depth of the black
abyss.   Their education was just on the eve of completion.

This is but a simple training, and for one of the inferior vocations.
There remains to speak of that of the arts: of the art of flight, the
art of song, the art of architecture.   Nothing is more complex than
the education of certain singing birds.   The perseverance of the
father, the docility of the young, are worthy of all admiration.

And this education extends beyond the family-circle.   The nightingales, the chaffinches, while still young or unskilful, know how to
listen to, and profit by, the superior bird which has been allotted to
them as their instructor.   In those Russian palaces where flourishes
the noble Oriental partiality for the bulbul's song, you see everywhere
these singing-schools.   The master nightingale, in his cage suspended
in the centre of a saloon, has his scholars ranged around him in their
respective cages.   A certain sum per hour is paid for each bird
brought here to learn his lesson.   Before the master sings they chatter
and gossip among themselves, salute and recognize one another.   But
as soon as the mighty teacher, with one imperious note, like that of
a sonorous steel bell, has imposed silence, you see them listen with a
sensible deference, then timidly repeat the strain.   The master com-
placently returns to the principal passages, corrects, and gently sets

them right. A few then grow bolder, and, by some felicitous chords, essay to supply the harmony to the dominant melody.

An education so delicate, so varied, so complex, is it that of a machine, of a brute reduced to instinct? Who can refuse in this to acknowledge a soul?

Open your eyes to the evidence. Throw aside your prejudices, your traditional and derived opinions. Preconceived ideas and dogmatic theories apart, you cannot offend Heaven by restoring a soul to the beast.* How much grander the Creator's work if he has created persons, souls, and wills, than if he has constructed machines!

Dismiss your pride, and acknowledge a kindred in which there is nothing to make a devout mind ashamed. What are these? They are your brothers.

What are they? embryo souls, souls especially set apart for certain functions of existence, candidates for the more general and more widely harmonic life to which the human soul has attained.

When will they arrive thither? and how? God has reserved to himself these mysteries.

All that we know is this: that he summons them—them also— to mount higher and yet higher.

* The reader must not identify the translator with these opinions, which, however, he did not feel at liberty to modify or omit.

They are, without metaphor, the little children of Nature, the nurslings of Providence, aspiring towards the light in order to act and think; stumbling now, they, by degrees, shall advance much further.

> " O pauvre enfantelet! du fil de tes pensées
> L'échevelet n'est encore débrouillé."

> Poor feeble child! not yet of thy thought's thread
> Is the entangled skein unravellèd.

Souls of children, in truth, but far gentler, more resigned, more patient than those of human children. See with what silent good humour most of them (like the horse) support blows, and wounds, and ill-treatment! They all know how to endure disease and suffer death. They retire apart, surround themselves with silence, and lie down in concealment; this gentle patience often supplies them with the most efficacious remedies. If not, they accept their destiny, and pass away as if they slept.

Can they love as deeply as we love? How shall we doubt it, when we see the most timid suddenly become heroic in defence of their young and their family? The devotedness of the man who braves death for his children you will see exemplified every day in the martin, which not only resists the eagle, but pursues him with heroical ardour.

Would you wish to observe two things wonderfully analogous? Watch on the one side the woman's delight at the first step of her infant, and on the other the swallow at the first flight of her little nursling.

You see in both the same anxiety, the same encouragements, examples, and counsels, the same pretended security and lurking fear, the trembling "Take courage, nothing is more easy;"—in truth, the two mothers are inwardly shivering.

The lessons are curious. The mother raises herself on her wings; the fledgling regards her intently, and also raises himself a little; then you see her hovering—he looks, he stirs his wings. All this goes well, for it takes place in the nest—the difficulty begins when he essays to quit it. She calls him, she shows him some little dainty tit-bit, she promises him a reward, she attempts to draw him forth with the bait of a fly.

Still the little one hesitates. And put yourself in his place. You have but to move a step in the nursery, between your nurse and your mother, where, if you fell, you would fall upon cushions. This bird of the church, which gives her first lesson in flying from the summit of the spire, can scarcely embolden her son, perhaps can scarcely embolden herself at the decisive moment. Both,—I am sure of it,—measure more than once with their glances the abyss beneath, and eye the ground. I, for one, declare to you, the spectacle is moving and sublime. It is an urgent need that he should *trust* his mother, that *she* should have confidence in the wing of the little one who is still a novice. From both does Heaven require an act of faith, of courage. A noble and a sublime starting-point! But he *has* trusted, he has made the leap, he will not fall. Trembling, he floats in air, supported by the paternal breath of heaven, by the re-assuring voice of his mother. All is finished. Thenceforth he will fly regardless of the wind and the storm, strong in that first great trial wherein he flew in faith.

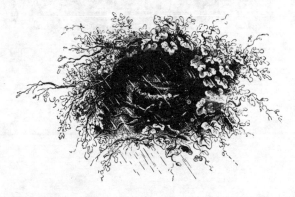

[NOTE.—*The Swallow's Flight.* According to Wilson, the swallow's ordinary flight averages one mile per minute. He is engaged in flying for ten hours daily. Now, as his life is usually extended to a space of ten years, he flies, in that period, 2,190,000 miles, or nearly eighty-eight times the circumference of the globe.

The swallow, as Sir Humphrey Davy observes, cheers the sense of sight as much as the nightingale does the sense of hearing. He is the glad prophet of the year, the harbinger of its brightest season, and lives a life of free enjoyment amongst the loveliest forms of nature.

There is something peculiarly beautiful in his rapid, steady, well-balanced flight,—

> " Which, ere a double pulse can beat,
> Is here and there with motion fleet,
> As Ariel's wing could scarce exceed;
> And, full of vigour as of speed,
> Forestalls the dayspring's earliest gleam,
> Nor fails with evening's latest beam."

To all nations he is welcome, and by all the poets has been celebrated with fond eulogium —*Translator.*]

THE NIGHTINGALE.

THE NIGHTINGALE.

ART AND THE INFINITE.

THE celebrated Pré-aux-Clercs, now known as the Marché Saint Germain, is, as everybody knows, on Sundays, the Bird Market of Paris. The place has more than one claim on our curiosity. It is a vast menagerie, frequently renewed—a shifting, strange museum of French ornithology.

On the other hand, such an auction of living beings, of captives many of whom feel their captivity, of slaves whom the auctioneer exposes, sells, and values more or less adroitly, indirectly reminds one, after all, of the markets of the East, the auctions of human slaves. The winged slaves, without understanding our languages, do not the less vividly express the thought of servitude; some, born in this condition, are resigned to it; others, sombre and silent, dream ever of freedom. Not a few appear to address themselves to you, seem desirous of arresting the passer-by's attention, and ask only for a good master. How often have we seen an intelligent goldfinch, an amiable robin, regarding us with a mournful gaze, but a gaze by no means doubtful in its meaning, for it said: "Buy me!"

One Sunday in summer we paid a visit to this mart, which we shall never forget. It was not well stocked, still less harmonious ; the season of moulting and of silence had begun. We were not the less keenly attracted by and interested in the naïve attitude of a few individuals. Ordinarily their song and their plumage, the bird's two principal attributes, preoccupy us, and prevent us from observing their lively and original pantomime. One bird, the American mocking-bird, has a comedian's genius, distinguishing all his songs by a mimicry strictly appropriate to their character, and often very ironical. Our birds do not possess this singular art ; but, without skill, and unknown to themselves, they express, by significant and frequently pathetic movements, the thoughts which traverse their brain.

On this particular day, the queen of the market was a black-capped warbler, an artist-bird of great value, set apart in the display from the other birds, like a peerless jewel. She fluttered, *svelte* and charming ; all in her was grace. Accustomed to captivity by a long training, she seemed to regret nothing, and could communicate to the soul only happy and gentle impressions. She was plainly a being of perfect geniality, and of such harmony of song and movement, that in seeing her move I thought I heard her sing.

Lower, very much lower, in a narrow cage, a bird somewhat larger in size, very inhumanly confined, gave me a curious and quite opposite impression. This was a chaffinch, and the first which I had seen blind. No spectacle could be more painful. The man who would purchase by such a deed of cruelty this victim's song, must have a nature alien to all harmony, a barbarous soul. His attitude of labour and torture rendered his song very painful to me. The worst of it is that it was human ; it reminded one of the turns of the head and the ungracious motions of the shoulders which short-sighted persons, or men become blind, indulge in. Such is never the case with those born blind. With a violent but continual effort, grown habitual, the head inclined to the right, with empty eyes he sought the light. The neck was outstretched, to sink again between the shoulders, and swelled out to gain new strength—the neck short, the shoulders bent.   This unhappy virtuoso, whose song, like himself, was dissembled and deformed, had been a mean image of the ugliness of the slave-artist, if not ennobled by that indomitable effort to pursue the light, seeking it always on high, and ever centering his song in the invisible sun which he had treasured up in his soul.

Moderately capable of profiting by instruction, this bird repeats, with a marvellous metallic *timbre*, the song of his native wood, and preserves the particular accent of the country in which he was born; there being as many dialects of chaffinches as there are different districts.   He remains faithful to his own; he sings only his cradle-song, and that with an uniform rate, but with a wild passion and an extraordinary emulation.   Set opposite a rival, he will repeat it eight hundred successive times; occasionally he dies of it.   I am not astonished that the Belgians enthusiastically celebrate the combats of this hero of the national song, the chorister of their forest of Ardennes, decreeing prizes, crowns, even triumphal arches, to those acts of supreme devotion in which life is yielded for victory.

Still lower down than the chaffinch, and in a very small and wretched cage, peopled pell-mell with half-a-dozen birds of very different sizes, I was shown a prisoner which I had not distinguished, a young nightingale caught that very morning. The fowler, by a skilful Machia-velism, had placed the little captive in a world of very joyous slaves, quite accustomed to their confinement. These were young troglodytes, recently born in a cage ; he had rightly calculated that the sight of the sports of innocent infancy sometimes beguiles great grief.

Great evidently, nay, overpowering, was his, and more impressive than any of those sorrows which we express by tears. A dumb agony, pent up within himself, and longing for the darkness. He had withdrawn into the shade as far as might be, to the bottom of the cage, half hidden in a small eating-trough, making himself large and swollen with his slightly-bristling feathers, closing his eyes, never opening them even when he was disturbed, shaken by the frolicsome and careless pastimes of the young turbulents, which frequently drove one another against him. Plainly he would neither see, nor hear, nor eat, nor console himself. These self-imposed shadows were, as I clearly saw, an effort, in his cruel suffering, *not to be*, an intentional suicide. With his mind he embraced death, and died, so far as he was able, by the suspension of his senses and of all external activity.

Observe that, in this attitude, there was no indication of malicious, bitter, or choleric feeling, nothing to remind one of his neighbour, the morose chaffinch, with his attitude of violent and torturing exertion. Even the indiscretion of the young birdlings which, without care or respect, occasionally threw themselves upon him, could call forth no mark of impatience. He said, obviously : " What matters it to one who is no more ? " Although his eyes were closed, I did not the less easily read him. I perceived an artist's soul, all tenderness and all light, without rancour and without harshness against the barbarity of the world and the ferocity of fate. And it was through this that he lived, through this that he could not die, because he found within himself, in his great sorrow, the all-powerful cordial inherent in his nature : *internal light, song.* In the language of nightingales, these two words convey the same meaning.

I comprehended that he did not die, because even then, despite himself, despite his keen desire of death, he could not do otherwise than sing. His heart chanted a voiceless strain, which I heard perfectly well:—

> " *Lascia che io pianga !*
> *La Libertà* "

Liberty!—Suffer me to weep!

I had not expected to find here once more that song which, in the old time, and by another mouth (a mouth which shall never again be opened), had already pierced my heart, and left a wound which no time shall efface.

I demanded of his custodian if he were for sale. The shrewd fellow replied that he was too young to be sold, that as yet he did not eat alone; a statement evidently untrue, for he was not that year's bird; but the man wished to keep him for disposal in the winter, when, his voice returning, he would fetch a higher price.

Such a nightingale, born in freedom, which alone is the true nightingale, bears a very different value from one born in a cage: he sings quite differently, having known liberty and nature, and regretting both. The better part of the great artist's genius is suffering.

Artist ! I have said the word, and I will not unsay it. This is not an analogy, a comparison of things having a resemblance : no, it is the thing itself.

The nightingale, in my opinion, is not the chief, but the only one, of the winged people to which this name can be justly given.

And why? He alone is a creator; he alone varies, enriches, amplifies his song, and augments it by new strains. He alone is fertile and diverse in himself; other birds are so by instruction and imitation. He alone resumes, contains almost all ; each of them, of the most brilliant, suggests a couplet to the nightingale.

Only one other bird, like him, attains sublime results in the bold and simple—I mean the lark, the daughter of the sun. And the nightingale also is inspired by the light ; so that, when in captivity, alone, and deprived of love, it suffices to unloose his song. Confined for a while in darkness, then suddenly restored to the day, he runs riot with enthusiasm, he bursts into hymns of joy. This difference, nevertheless, exists between the two birds : the lark never sings in the night; hers is not the nocturnal melody, the hidden meaning of the grand effects of evening, the deep poesy of the shadows, the solemnity of midnight, the aspirations before dawn —in a word, that infinitely varied poem which translates and reveals to us, in all its changes, a great heart brimful of tenderness. The lark's is the lyrical genius; the nightingale's, the epic, the drama, the inner struggle,—from thence, a light apart.   In deep darkness, he looks into his soul, into love ; soaring at times, it would seem, beyond the individual love into the ocean of love infinite.

And will you not call him an artist ? He has the artist's temperament, and exalted to a degree which man himself rarely attains. All which belongs to it—all its merits, all its defects—in him are superabundant. He is mild and timid, mistrustful, but not at all cunning. He takes no heed to his safety, and travels alone. He is burningly jealous, equalling the chaffinch in fiery emulation.   "He will break his heart to sing," says one of his historians.*   He listens ; he takes up his abode, especially where an echo exists, to listen and

reply. Nervous to an excess, one sees him in captivity sometimes sleeping long through the day with perturbing dreams ; sometimes

* Everybody knows the beautiful story of the " Musician's Duel "—the rivalry between a nightingale and a flute-player--as told by Ford and Crashaw.—*Translator*

struggling, starting up, and wildly battling.   He is subject to nervous attacks and epilepsy.

He is kindly—he is ferocious.   Let me explain myself.   His heart is full of tenderness for the weak and little.   Give him orphans to watch over, he will take charge of them, and clasp them to his heart; a male, and aged, he nourishes and tends them as carefully as any mother-bird.   On the other hand, he is exceedingly cruel towards his prey, is greedy and voracious; the flame which burns inly, and keeps him almost always thin, makes him constantly feel the need of recruitment, and it is also one of the reasons that he is so easily ensnared.   It is enough to set your bait in the morning; especially in April and May, when he exhausts himself by singing throughout the night.   In the morning, weakened, frail, avid, he pounces blindly on the snare.   Moreover, he is very curious, and, in order to examine a novel object, will expose himself to be caught.

Once captured, if you do not take the precaution to tie his wings, or rather to cover the interior and pad the upper part of the cage, he will kill himself by the frantic fury of his movements.

This violence is on the surface.   At bottom, he is gentle and docile : it is these qualities which raise him so high, and make him in truth an artist.   He is not only the most inspired, but the most tractable, the most " civilizable," the most laborious of birds.

It is a charming sight to see the fledglings gathered round their father, listening to him attentively, and profiting by his lessons to form the voice, to correct their faults, to soften their novice-like roughness, to render their young organs supple.

But how much more curious it is to see him training himself, judging, perfecting himself, paying especial attention when he ventures on new themes !   This steadfast perseverance, which springs from his reverence for his art and from a kind of inward religion, is the morality of the artist, his divine consecration, which seals him as one apart—distinguishes him from the vain improvisatore, whose unconscientious babble is a simple echo of nature.

Thus love and light are undoubtedly his point of departure ; but art itself, the love of the beautiful, confusedly seen in glimpses, and very keenly felt, are a second aliment, which sustains his soul, and supplies it with a new inspiration.   And this is boundless—a day opened on the infinite.

The true greatness of the artist consists in overshooting his mark, in doing more than he willed ; and, moreover, in passing far beyond the goal, in crossing the limits of the possible, and looking beyond— beyond.

Hence arise great sorrows, an inexhaustible source of melancholy ; hence the sublime folly of weeping over misfortunes which he has never experienced.   Other birds are astonished, and occasionally inquire of him what is the cause of his grief, what does he regret. When free and joyous in his forest-home, he does not the less vouch-safe for his reply the strain which my captive chanted in his silence :

" Lascia che io pianga ! "

Suffer me, suffer me to weep !

THE NIGHTINGALE.

THE NIGHTINGALE:

CONTINUED.

THE hours of silence are not barren for the nightingale. He gathers his ideas and reflects; he broods over the songs which he has heard or has himself attempted; he modifies and improves them with perfect tact and taste. For the false notes of an ignorant master he substitutes ingenious and harmonious variations. The imperfect strain which he has learned, but has not repeated, he then reproduces; but made indeed his own, appropriated by his own genius, and converted into a nightingale's melody.

"Do not be discouraged," says a quaint old writer "if the young bird be not willing to repeat your lesson, and continue to warble; soon he will show you that he has not forgotten the lessons received in autumn and winter—*a fit season for meditation, owing to the length of the nights;* he will repeat them in the spring-time."

It is very interesting to follow, during the winter, the nightingale's thoughts, in his darkened cage, wrapped round with a green cloth, which partially deceives his gaze, and reminds him of his forest. In December he begins to dream aloud, to descant, to describe in pathetic notes the things passing before his mind—the loved and absent objects. Mayhap he then forgets that migration has been forbidden him, and thinks he has arrived in Africa or in Syria, in lands lighted by a more generous sun. It may be that he sees this sun; sees the rose reblossom, and recommences for her, as say the Persian poets, his hymn of impossible love,—" *O sun ! O sea ! O rose !*"- (*Rückert.*)

For myself, I believe simply that this noble and pathetic hymn, with its lofty accent, is nought else but himself, his life of love and combat, his nightingale's drama. He beholds the woods, the beloved object which transfigures them. He sees her tender vivacity, and the thousand graces of the winged life which we are unable to perceive. He speaks to her; she answers him. He takes upon himself two characters, and, to the full, sonorous voice of the male, replies in soft, brief utterances. What then? I doubt not that already the rapturousness of his life breaks upon him—the tender intimacy of the nest, the little lowly dwelling which would have been his Eden. He believes in it; he shuts his eyes, and completes the illusion. The egg is hatched; his Yule-tide miracle disclosed; his son issues forth—the future nightingale, even at its birth sublimely melodious. He listens ecstatically, in the night of his gloomy cage, to the future song of his offspring.

And all this, to be sure, passes before him in a poetical confusion, where obstacles and strife break up and disturb love's festival. No happiness here below is pure. A *third* intervenes. The captive in his solitude grows irritated and eager; he struggles visibly against his unseen adversary—*that other*, the unworthy rival which is present to his mind.

The scene is developed before him, just as it would have transpired in spring, when the male birds returning, towards March or April, and before the re-appearance of the hens, resolve to decide among themselves their great duel of jealousy. For when the latter arrive, all must be calm and peaceful; there should prevail nothing but love, tranquillity, and tenderness. The battle endures some fifteen days; and if the female birds return sooner, the effort grows deadly. The story of Roland is literally realized; he sounded his ivory horn, even to the extinction of strength and life. These, too, sing until their last breath——until death: they will triumph or die.

If it be true, as we are assured, that the lovers are two or three times more numerous than the lady-loves, you may conceive the violence of this burning emulousness, in which, perhaps, lurks the first spark and the secret of their genius.

The fate of the vanquished is terrible—worse than death. He is constrained to fly; to quit the province, the country; to sink into the comrade of the lower races of birds; while his song is degraded into a *patois*. He forgets and disgraces himself; becomes vulgarized among this vulgar people; little by little growing ignorant of his own tongue, of theirs, of any tongue. We sometimes discover among these exiles birds which preserve only the external likeness of the nightingale.

Though the rival is expelled, nothing as yet is done. The victor must please, must subdue her. Oh! bright moment, soft inspiration of the new song which shall touch that little proud Wild-heart, and compel it to abandon liberty for love! The test imposed by the hen-bird in other species is assistance in building or excavating the nest; that the male may show he is skilful, and will take his offspring to his heart. The effect is sometimes admirable. The woodpecker, as we have seen, is elevated from a workman into an artist, and from a carpenter into a sculptor. But, alas! the nightingale does not possess this talent; he is ignorant of all kinds of labour. The least among the small birds is a hundred times more adroit with his bill, his wing, his claw. He has only his voice which he can make use of; there his power breaks forth, there he will be irresistible. Others may display their works, but his work is himself; he shows, he reveals himself, and he appears sublime and grand.

I have never heard him at this solemn moment without thinking that not only should he touch her heart, but transform, ennoble, and exalt her, inspire her with a lofty ideal, with the enchanted dream of a glorious nightingale which shall be hereafter the offspring of their love.

Let us resume. So far, we have particularized three songs.

The drama of the battle-song, with its alternations of envy, pride, bravado, stern and jealous fury.

The song of solicitation, of soft and tender entreaty, but mingled with haughty movements of an almost imperious impatience, wherein genius is visibly astonished that it still remains unrecognized, is irritated at the delay, and laments it ; returning quickly, however, to its tone of reverent pleading.

Finally comes the song of triumph : "I am the conqueror, I am loved, the king, the divinity, and the creator." In this last word lies all the intensity of life and love ; for it is she, above all, that creates, mirroring and reflecting his genius, and so transforming herself that henceforth there is not in her a movement, a breath, a flutter of the wings, which does not owe its melodiousness to him, rendered visible in this enchanted grace.

Thence spring the nest, the egg, the infant. All these are an embodied and living song. And this is the reason that he does not stir from her for a moment, during the sacred labour of incubation. He does not remain in the nest, but on a neighbouring branch, slightly elevated above it. He knows marvellously well that his voice is most potent at a distance. From this exalted position, the all-powerful magician continues to fascinate and fertilize the nest; he co-operates in the great mystery, and still inspires with song, and heart, and breath, and will, and tenderness.

This is the time that you should hear him, should hear him in his native woods, should participate in the emotions of this powerful fecundity, the most proper perhaps to reveal, to enable us to comprehend here below the great hidden Deity which eludes us. He recedes before us at every step, and science does no more than put a little further back the veil wherein he conceals himself. "Behold," said Moses, "behold him who passes, I have seen him by the skirts." "Is it not he," said Linné, "who passes? I have seen him in outline." And for myself, I close my eyes; I perceive him with an agitated heart, I feel him stirring within me on a night enchanted by the voice of the nightingale.

Let us draw near; it is a lover: yet keep you distant, for it is a god. The melody, now vibrating with a glowing appeal to the senses, anon grows sublime and amplified by the effects of the wind; it is a strain of sacred harmony which swells through all the forest. Near at hand, it is occupied with the nest, their love, the son which will be born; but afar, another is the beloved, another is the son: it is Nature, mother and daughter, eternal love, which hymns and glorifies itself; it is the infinite of love which loves in all things and sings in all; these are the tendernesses, the canticles, the songs of gratitude, which go up from earth to heaven.

*　　*　　*　　*

"Child, I have felt this in our southern fields, during the beautiful starry nights, near my father's house. At a later time, I felt it more keenly, especially in the vicinity of Nantes, in the lonesome vineyard of which I have spoken in a preceding page. The nights, less sparkling, were lightly veiled with a warm haze, through which the stars discreetly sent their tender glances. A nightingale nestled on the ground, in a spot but half concealed, under my cedar tree, and among the periwinkle-flowers. He began towards midnight, and continued until dawn; happily, manifestly proud, in his solitary vigil, and filling the majestic silence with his voice. No one interrupted him except, near morning, the cock, a creature of a different world, a stranger to the songs of the spirit, but a punctual sentinel, who felt himself conscientiously compelled to indicate the hour and warn the workman.

"The other persisted for some time in his strain, seeming to say, like Juliet to Romeo: 'No, it is not the day.'

"His stationing himself near us showed that he feared nothing, that he knew how profound a security he might enjoy by the side of two hermits of work, very busy, very benevolent, and not less occupied than the winged solitary in their song and their dream. We could watch him at our ease, either fluttering about en famille, or maintaining a rivalry in song with a haughty neighbour who sometimes came to brave him. In course of time we became, I think, rather agreeable to him, as assiduous auditors, amateurs, perhaps connoisseurs. The nightingale feels the want of appreciation and applause; he plainly has a great regard for man's attentive ear, and fully comprehends his admiration.

"Once more I can see him, at some ten or fifteen paces distant, hopping forward in accordance with my movements, preserving the same interval between us, so as to keep always out of reach, but at the same time to be heard and admired.

"The attire in which you are clothed is by no means a matter of indifference to him. I have observed that birds in general do not like black, and that they are afraid of it. I was dressed quite to his fancy, in white shaded with lilac, with a straw hat ornamented with a few blossoms. Every minute I could see him fix upon me his black eye, of a singular vivacity, wild and gentle, sometimes a little proud,

which said plainly, 'I am free, and I have wings; against me thou
canst do nothing.   But I am very willing to sing for thee.'

"We had a succession of severe storms at breeding-time, and on
one occasion the thunder rolled near us.   No scene can be more
affecting than the approach of these moments: the air fails; fish rise
to the surface in order to breathe a little; the flower bends languidly;
everything suffers, and tears flow unbidden.   I could see clearly that
his feelings were in unison with the general distress.   From his
bosom, oppressed like mine, broke a kind of hoarse sob, like a
wild cry.

"But the wind, which had suddenly risen, now plunged into our
woods; the loftiest trees, even the cedar, bent.   Torrents of rain
dashed headlong, all was afloat.   What became of the poor little nest,
exposed on the ground, with no other shelter than the periwinkle's
leaf?   It escaped; for when the sun reappeared, I saw my bird
flying in the purified air, gayer than ever, with his heart full of
song.   All the world of wings then hymned the light; but he more
loudly than any.   His clarion voice had returned.   I saw him beneath my window, his eye on fire and his breast swollen, intoxi-

cating himself with the same happiness that made my heart palpitate.

"Tender alliance of souls! Why does it not everywhere exist, between us and our winged brothers, between man and the universal living nature?"

CONCLUSION.

CONCLUSION.

At the very moment that I am about to pen the conclusion of this book, our illustrious master arrives from his great autumnal sport. Toussenel brings me a nightingale.

I had requested him to assist me with his advice, to guide me in choosing a singing nightingale. He does not write, but he comes; he does not advise, he looks about, finds, gives, realizes my dream. This, of a truth, is friendship.

Be welcome, bird, both for the sake of the cherished hand which brings thee, and for thy own, for thy hallowed muse, the genius which dwells within thee!

Wilt thou sing readily for me, and, by thy puissance of love and calm, shed harmony on a heart troubled by the cruel history of men?

It was an event in our family, and we established the poor artist-prisoner in a window-niche, but enveloped with a curtain; in such wise that, being both in solitude and yet in society, he might gradually accustom himself to his new hosts, reconnoitre the locality, and assure himself that he was under a safe, a peaceful, and benevolent roof.

No other bird lived in this saloon. Unfortunately, my familiar robin, which flies freely about my study, penetrated into the apartment.   We had troubled ourselves the less about him, because he saw daily, without any emotion, canaries, bullfinches, nightingales; but the sight of the nightingale threw him into an incredible transport of fury.   Passionate and intrepid, without heeding that the object of his hate was twice his own size, he pounced on the cage with bill and claws; he would fain have killed its inmate.   The nightingale, however, uttered cries of alarm, and called for help with a hoarse and pitiful voice.   The other, checked by the bars, but clinging with his claws to the frame of an adjacent picture, raged, hissed, *crackled* (the popular word *petillait* alone expresses his short, sharp cry), piercing him with his glances.   He said, in effect:—

"King of song, what dost thou here?   Is it not enough that in the woods thy imperious and absorbing voice should silence all our lays, hush our strains into whispers, and singly fill the desert? Yet thou comest hither to deprive me of the new existence which I have found for myself, of this artificial grove where I perch all the winter, a grove whose branches are the shelves of a library, whose leaves are books !   Thou comest to share, to usurp the attention of which I was the object, the reverie of my master, and my mistress's smile !   Woe to thee !   I *was* loved !"

The robin does, in reality, attain to a very high degree of familiarity with man.   The experience of a long winter proves to me that he much prefers human society to that of his own kind.   In our absence he shares in the small talk of the birds of the aviary; but as soon as we arrive, he abandons them, and comes curiously to place himself before us, remains with us, seems to say, "You are here, then! But where have you been? And why have you absented yourself so long from home?"

The invasion of the robin, which we soon forgot, was not forgotten, it appears, by his timorous victim. The unfortunate nightingale fluttered about ever afterwards with an air of alarm, and nothing could reassure him.

Care was taken, however, that no one should approach him. His mistress had charged herself with the necessary attentions. The peculiar mixture which alone can nourish this ardent centre of life (blood, hemp, and poppy), was conscientiously prepared. Blood and flesh, these are the substance; hemp is the herb of intoxication; but the poppy neutralizes it. The nightingale is the only creature which it is necessary to feed incessantly with sleep and dreams.

But all was in vain. Two or three days passed in a violent agitation, and in abstinence through despair. I was melancholy, and filled with remorse. I, a friend of freedom, had nevertheless a prisoner, and a prisoner who would not be consoled! It was not without some scruples that I had formed the idea of procuring a nightingale; for the mere sake of pleasure, I should never have come to such a decision. I knew well that the very spectacle of such a captive, deeply sensible of its captivity, was a permanent source of sorrow. But how should I set him free? Of all questions, that of slavery is the most difficult; the tyrant is punished by the impossibility of finding a remedy for it. My captive, before coming into my possession, had been two years in a cage, and had neither wings nor the impulse of industry to seek his own food; but had it been otherwise, he could return no more to the free birds. In their proud commonwealth, whoever has been a slave, whoever has languished in a cage and not died of grief, is pitilessly condemned and put to death.

We should not easily have escaped from this dilemma, if song had not come to our assistance. A soft, almost monotonous strain,

sung at a distance, especially just before evening, appeared to influence and win upon him.   If we did but look at him, he listened less
attentively, and grew disturbed; but if we turned aside our gaze, he
came to the brink of the cage, stretched out his long, fawn-like neck
(of a charming mouse-like gray), raised every now and then his head,
his body remaining motionless, with a keen inquiring eye.   With
evident avidity, he tasted and enjoyed this unexpected pleasure, with
grateful recollection, and delicate and sensitive attention.

This same avidity he felt a minute afterwards for his food.   He
was fain to live, he devoured the poppy, forgetfulness.

A woman's songs, Toussenel had told me, are those which affect
them most; not the vivacious aria of a wayward damsel, but a soft,
sad melody.   Schubert's " Serenade " had a peculiar influence upon
our nightingale.   He seemed to feel and recognize himself in that
German soul, as tender as it was profound.

His voice, however, he did not regain.   When transported to my
house, he had begun his December songs.   The emotions of the
journey, the change of *locale* and of persons, the inquietude which he
had experienced in his new condition, and, above all, the ferocious
welcome, the robin's assault, had too deeply moved him.   He
grew tranquil, asked no more of us; but the muse, so rudely
interrupted, was thenceforth silent, and did not awake until
Spring.

Meanwhile, he certainly knew that the person who sang afar off
wished him no evil; he apparently supposed her to be a nightingale
of another form.   She might without difficulty approach, and even
put her hand in his cage.   He regarded intently what she did, but
did not stir.

It became a curious question to me, who had not contracted with
him this musical alliance, to know if he would also accept me.   I
showed no indiscreet eagerness, knowing that even a look, at certain
moments, vexes him.   For many days, therefore, I kept my attention
fixed on the old books or papers of the fourteenth century, without
observing him.   But he, he would examine me very curiously when

I was alone. Be it understood, however, that when his mistress was present, he entirely forgot me, I was annulled !

Thus he grew accustomed to see me daily without any uneasiness, as an inoffensive, pacific being, with little of movement or noise about me. The fire in the grate, and near the fire this peaceable reader, were, during the absences of the preferred individual, in the still and almost solitary hours, his objects of contemplation.

I ventured yesterday, being alone, to approach him, to speak to him as I do to the robin, and he did not grow agitated, he did not appear disturbed ; he listened quietly, with an eye full of softness.   I saw that peace was concluded, and that I was accepted.

This morning I have with my own hand placed the poppy seed in the cage, and he is not the least alarmed. You will say : " Who gives is welcome." But I assert that our treaty was signed yesterday, before I had given him anything, and was perfectly disinterested.

See, then, in less than a month, the most nervous of artists, the most timid and mistrustful of beings, grows reconciled with the human species.

A curious proof of the natural union, of the pre-existent alliance which prevails between us and these creatures of instinct, which we call *inferior*.

This alliance, this eternal fact, which our brutality and our ferocious intelligences have not yet been able to rend asunder, to which these poor little ones so readily return, to which we shall

ourselves return, when we shall be truly men, is exactly the conclusion this book has aimed at, and which I was about to write,
when the nightingale entered, and the father with the nightingale.

The bird himself has been, in that facile amnesty which he has
granted to us, his tyrants, my living conclusion.

————————

Those travellers who have been the first to penetrate into lands
hitherto untrodden by man, unanimously report that all animals,
mammals, amphibians, birds, do not shun them, but, on the contrary,
rather approach to regard them with an air of benevolent curiosity,
to which they have responded with musket-shots.

Even to-day, after man has treated them so cruelly, animals,
in their times of peril, never hesitate to draw near him.

The bird's ancient and natural foe is the serpent; the enemy of
quadrupeds is the tiger.   And their protector is man.

From the furthest distance that the wild dog smells the scent of
the tiger or the lion, he comes to press close to us.

And so, too, the bird, in the horror which the serpent inspires,
especially when it threatens his callow brood, finds a language of the
most forcible character to implore man's help, and to thank him if he
kills his enemy.

For this reason the humming-bird loves to nestle near man.
And it is probably from the same motive that the swallows and the

storks, in times fertile in reptiles, have acquired the habit of dwelling among us.

Here an observation becomes essential. We often construe as a sign of mistrust the bird's flight and his fear of the human hand. This fear is only too well founded. But even if it did not exist, the bird is an infinitely nervous and delicate creature, which suffers if simply touched.

My robin, which belongs to a very robust and friendly race of birds, which continually draws near us, as near as possible, and which assuredly has no fear of his mistress, trembles to fall into her hand. The rustling of his plumes, the derangement of his down, all bristling when he has been handled, he keenly dislikes. The sight, above all, of the outstretched hand about to seize him, makes him recoil instinctively.

When he lingers about in the evening, and does not return into his cage, he does not refuse to be replaced within it; but sooner than see himself caught, he turns his back, hides in a crease or fold of the gown where he well knows he must infallibly be taken.

All this is not mistrust.

———————

The art of domestication will make no progress if it occupies itself only with the services which tamed animals may render to man.

It ought to proceed in the main from the consideration of the service which man may render the animals;

Of his duty to initiate all the tenants of this world into a gentler, more peaceable, and superior society.

———————

In the barbarism in which we are still plunged, we know of only two conditions for the animal, absolute liberty or absolute slavery:

but there are many forms of demi-servitude which the animals themselves would willingly accept.

The small Chili falcon (*cernicula*), for example, loves to dwell
with his master.   He goes alone on his hunting expeditions, and
faithfully returns every evening with what he has captured, to eat it
en famille.   He feels the want of being praised by the father, flattered
by the dame, and, above all, caressed by the children.

Man, formerly protected by the animals, while he was indifferently
armed, has gradually risen into a position to become their protector,
especially since he has had powder, and enjoyed the possibility of
shooting down from a distance the most formidable creatures.   He has
rendered birds the essential service of infinitely diminishing the number
of the robbers of the air.

He may render them another, and not a less important one—that
of sheltering at night the innocent species.   Night! sleep! complete
abandonment to the most frightful chances!   Oh! harshness of
Nature!   But she is justified, inasmuch as she has planted here
below the far-seeing and industrious being who shall more and more
become for all others a second providence.

"I know a house on the Indre," says Toussenel, "where the
greenhouses, open at even, receive every honest bird which seeks an
asylum against the dangers of the night, where he who has delayed
till late knocks with his bill in confidence.   Content to be immured

during the night, secure in the loyalty of their host, they fly away happy in the morning, and repay him for his hospitality with the spectacle of their joy and their unrestricted strains."

I shall exercise great caution in speaking of their domestication, since my friend, M. Isidore Geoffrey Saint Hilaire, reopens in so praiseworthy a manner this long-forgotten question.

An allusion will suffice. Antiquity in this special branch has bequeathed us the admirable patrimony which has supported the human race : the domestication of the dog, the horse, and the ass ; of the camel, the elephant, the ox, the sheep, the goat, and poultry.

What progress has been made in the last two thousand years ? What new acquisition ?

Two only, and these unquestionably trivial : the importation of the turkey and the China pheasant.

No direct effort of man has accomplished so much for the welfare of the globe as the humble toil of the modest auxiliaries of human life.

To descend to that which we so foolishly despise, to the poultry-yard, when one sees the millions of eggs which the ovens of Egypt hatch, or with which our Normandy loads the ships and fleets that every year traverse the Channel, one learns to appreciate how the small agencies of domestic economy produce the greatest results.

If France did not possess the horse, and some person introduced it, such a conquest would be of greater benefit to her than the conquest of the Rhine, of Belgium, of Savoy ; the horse alone would be worth three kingdoms.

But here now is an animal which represents in itself the horse, the ass, the cow, the goat ; which combines all their useful qualities, and which yields moreover an incomparable wool ; a hardy, robust animal, enduring cold with wonderful vigour. You understand, of course, that I refer to the lama, which M. Isidore Geoffrey Saint Hilaire exerts himself, with so laudable a perseverance, to naturalize in France. Everything seems leagued in his despite : the fine flock at Versailles has perished through malice ; that of the Jardin des Plantes will perish through the confined area and dampness of the locality.

The conquest of the lama is ten times more important than the conquest of the Crimea.

But again, this species of transplantation needs a generosity of means, a combination of precautions, let us say a tenderness of education, which are rarely found united.

One word here—one small fact—whose bearing is not small.

A great writer, who was not a man of science, Bernardin de Saint Pierre, had remarked that we should never succeed in transplanting the animal unless we imported along with him the plant to which he was especially partial. This observation fell to the ground, like so many other theories which excite the philosophical smile, and which men of science name *poetry*.

But it has not been made in vain, for an enlightened amateur had formed here, in Paris, a collection of living birds. However constant his attentions, a very rare she-parrot which he had obtained remained obstinately barren. He ascertained in what kind of plant she made her nest, and commissioned a person to procure it for him.

It could not be got alive; he received it leafless and branchless; a simple dead trunk. It mattered not; the bird, in this hollow trunk, discovered her accustomed place, and did not fail to make therein her nest. She laid eggs, she hatched them, and now her owner has a colony of young ones.

To re-create all the conditions of abode, food, vegetable environment, the harmonies of every kind which shall deceive the exile into a forgetfulness of his country, is not only a scientific question, but a task of ingenious invention.

To determine the limit of slavery, of freedom, of alliance and collaboration with ourselves, proper for each individual creature, is one of the gravest subjects which can occupy us.

A new art is this; nor shall you succeed in it without a moral gravity, a refinement, a delicacy of appreciation which as yet are scarcely understood, and shall exist, perhaps, only when Woman undertakes those scientific studies from which she has hitherto been excluded.

This art supposes a tenderness unlimited in justice and wisdom.

ILLUSTRATIVE NOTES.

ILLUSTRATIVE NOTES.

THE chief illustration of a book is incontestably the formula in which it is summed up. Here it is, then, in few words :—

This book has considered the bird *in himself*, and but little in relation to man.

The bird, born in a much lower condition than man (oviparous, like the serpent), possesses three advantages over him, which are his special mission :—

I. *The wing, flight,* an unique power, which is the dream of man. Every other creature is slow. Compared with the falcon or swallow, the Arab horse is a snail.

II. Flight itself does not appertain solely to the wing, but to an incomparable power of *respiration and vision.* The bird is peculiarly the son of air and light.

III. An essentially electrical being, *the bird sees, knows, and foresees earth and sky, the weather, the seasons.* Whether through an intimate relation with the globe, whether through a prodigious memory of localities and routes, he is always facing eastward, and always knows his path.

He swoops; he penetrates; he attains what man shall never attain. This is evident, particularly in his marvellous war against the reptile and the insect.

Add the marvellous work of continual purification of everything dangerous and unclean, which some species accomplish. If this war and this work ceased but for one day, man would disappear from the earth.

This daily victory of the beloved son of light over death, over a murderous and tenebrous life, is the fitting theme of his *song*, of that hymn of joy with which the bird salutes each Dawn.

But, besides song, the bird has many other languages. Like man, he prattles, recites, converses. He and man are the only beings which have really a language. Man and the bird are the voice of the world.

The bird, with its gift of augury, is ever drawing near to man, who is ever inflicting injury upon him. He undoubtedly divines, and has a presentiment of, what man will one day become when he emerges from the barbarism in which he is now unhappily plunged.

He recognizes in him the creature unique, sanctified, and blessed, who ought to be the arbiter of all, who should accomplish the destiny of this globe by one supreme act of good—the union of all life and the reconciliation of all beings.

This pacific union must after a time be effected by a great art of education and initiation, which man begins to comprehend.

Page 64. *Training for flight* (see also p. 84).—Is it wrong for man, in his reveries, to beguile himself into a belief that he will one day be more than man, to attribute to himself wings? Dream or presentiment, it matters not.

It is certain that a power of flight such as the bird possesses is truly a *sixth sense*. It would be absurd to see in it only an auxiliary of touch.　(See, among other works, Huber, *Vol des oiseaux de proie*, 1784).

The wing is so rapid and so infallible only because it is aided by a visual faculty which has not its equal in all creation.

The bird, we must confess, lives wholly in the air, in the light. If there be a sublime life, a life of fire, it is this.

Who surveys and descries all earth ?　Who measures it with his glance and his wing ?　Who knows all its paths ?　And not in any beaten route, but at the same time in every direction : for where is not the bird's track ?

His relations with heat, electricity, and magnetism, all the imponderable forces, are scarcely known to us ; we see them, however, in his singular meteorological prescience.

If we had seriously studied the matter, we should have had the balloon some thousands of years ago ; but even with the balloon, and the balloon capable of being *steered*, we should still be enormously behind the bird.　To imitate its mechanism, and exactly reproduce its details, is not to possess the agreement, the *ensemble*, the unity of action, which moves the whole with so much facility and with such terrible swiftness.

Let us renounce, for this life at least, these higher gifts, and confine ourselves to examine the two machines—our own and the bird's—in those points where they differ least.

The human machine is superior in what is its smallest peculiarity, its susceptibility of adaptation to the most diverse purposes, and, above all, in its all-powerful hand.

On the other hand, he has far less unity and centralization.　Our inferior limbs, our thighs and legs, which are very long, perform eccentric movements far from the central point of action.　Circulation is very slow ; a thing perceptible in those last moments, when the body is dead at the feet before the heart has ceased to throb.

The bird, almost spherical in form, is certainly the apex, divine and sublime, of living centralization.　We can neither see nor imagine a higher degree of unity.　From his excess of concentration he derives his great personal force, but it implies his extreme individuality, his isolation, his social weakness.

The profound, the marvellous solidarity, which is found in the higher genera of insects, as in the bees and ants, is not discovered among birds. Flocks of them are common, but true republics are rare.

Family ties are very strong in their influence, such as maternity and love. Brotherhood, the sympathy of species, the mutual assistance rendered even by different kinds, are not unknown. Nevertheless, fraternity is strong among them in the inferior line. The whole heart of the bird is in his love, in his nest.

There lies his isolation, his feebleness, his dependence; there also the temptation to seek for himself a defender.

The most exalted of living beings is not the less one of those which the most eagerly demand protection.

Page 67. *On the life of the bird in the egg.*—I draw these details from the accurate M. Duvernoy. Ovology in our days has become a science. Yet I know but a few treatises specially devoted to the bird's egg. The oldest is that of an Abbé Manesse, written in the last century, very verbose, and not very instructive (the MS. is preserved in

the Museum Library). The same library possesses the German work of Wirfing and Gunther on nests and eggs; and another, also German, whose illustrations appear of a superior character, although still defective. I have seen a part of a new collection of engravings, much more carefully executed.

Page 14. *Gelatinous and nourishing seas.*—Humboldt, in one of his early works ("Scenes in the Tropics"), was the first, I think, to authenticate this fact. He attributes it to the prodigious quantity of medusæ, and other analogous creatures, in a decomposed state in these waters. If, however, such a cadaverous dissolution really prevailed there, would it not render the waters fatal to the fish, instead of nourishing them? Perhaps this phenomenon should be attributed rather to nascent life than to life extinct, to that first living fermentation in which the lowest microscopic organizations develop themselves.

It is especially in the Polar Seas, whose aspect is so wild and desolate, that this characteristic is observed. Life there abounds in such excess that the colour of the waters is completely changed by it. They are of an intense olive-green, thick with living matter and nutriment.

Page 91. *Our Museum.*—In speaking of its collections, I may not forget its valuable library, which now includes that of Cuvier, and has been enriched by donations from all the physicists of Europe. I

have had occasion to acknowledge very warmly the courtesy of the conservator, M. Desnoyers, and of M. le Docteur Lemercier, who has obligingly supplied me with a number of pamphlets and curious memoirs from his private collection.

Page 94. *Buffon.*—I think that now-a-days we too readily forget that this great *generalizer* has not the less received and recorded a number of very accurate observations furnished him by men of special vocations, officers of the royal hunt, gamekeepers, marines, and persons of every profession.

Page 96. *The Penguin.*—The brother of the auk, but less degraded; he carries his wings like a veritable bird, though they are only membranes floating on an evoided breast. The more rarified air of our northern pole, where he lives, has already expanded his lungs, and the breast-bone begins to project. The legs, less closely confined to the body, better maintain its equilibrium, and the port and attitude gain in confidence. There is here a notable difference between the analogous products of the two hemispheres.

Page 103. *The Petrel, the mariner's terror.*—The legend of the petrel gliding upon the waves, around the ship which he appears to lead to perdition, is of Dutch origin. This is just as it ought to be. The Dutch, who voyage *en famille*, and carry with them their wives, their children, even their domestic animals, have been more susceptible to evil auguries than other navigators. The hardiest of all, perhaps—true amphibians—they have not the less been anxious and imaginative, hazarding not only their lives, but their affections,

and exposing to the fantastic chances of the sea the beloved home, a world of tenderness. That small lumbering bark, which is in truth a floating house, will nevertheless go, ever rolling across the seas of the North, the great Arctic Ocean, and the furious Baltic, accomplishing without pause the most dangerous voyages, as from Amsterdam to Cronstadt. We laugh at these ugly vessels and their antiquated build, but he who observes how plenteously they combine the two purposes of store-room for the cargo and accommodation for the family, can never see them in the ports of Holland without a lively interest, or without lavishing on them his good wishes.

Page 113. *Epiornis.*—The remains of this gigantic bird and its enormous egg may be seen in the Museum. It is computed that its size was fivefold that of the ostrich. How much we must regret that our rich collection of fossils, or the major part, lies buried in the drawers of the Museum for want of room. For thirty or forty thousand francs a wooden gallery might be constructed, in which the whole could find opportunities of display.

Meanwhile, we argue as if these vast studies, now in their very infancy, had already been exhausted. Who knows but that man has seen only the threshold of the prodigious world of the dead? He has scarcely scratched the surface of the globe. The deeper explorations to which he is constrained by the thousand novel needs of art and industry (as that, for example, of piercing the Alps for a new railway) will open to science unexpected prospects. Palæontology as yet is built upon the narrow foundation of a *minimum* number of facts. If we remember that the dead—owing to the thousands of years the globe has already lived—are enormously more numerous than the living, we cannot but consider this method of reasoning

upon a few specimens very audacious.   It is a hundred, nay, a thousand to one, that so many millions of dead, once disinterred, will con-
vict us of having erred, at least, through *incomplete enumeration.*

Page 113. *Man had perished a hundred times.*—Here we trace
one of the early causes of the limited confederacy originally existing
between man and the animal—a compact forgotten by our ungrateful
pride, and without which, nevertheless, the existence of man had
been impossible.

When the colossal birds whose remains we are constantly exhuming
had prepared for him the globe, had subjugated the crawling, climbing
life which at first predominated—when man came upon the earth to
confront what remained of the reptiles, to confront those new but not
less formidable inhabitants of our planet, the tiger and the lion—he
found on his side the bird, the dog, and the elephant.

At Alexandria may be seen the last few individuals of those
giant dogs which could strangle a lion.   It was not through terror
that these formidable animals allied themselves with man, but
through natural sympathy, and their peculiar antipathy to the feline
race, the giant cat (the tiger or lion).

Without the alliance of the dog against beasts of prey, and that
of the bird against serpents and crocodiles (which the bird kills in
the very egg), man had assuredly been lost.

The useful friendship of the horse originated in the same cause.
You may trace it in the indescribable and convulsive horror which
every young horse experiences at the mere odour of the lion.   He
attaches and surrenders himself to man.

Had he not possessed the horse, the ox, and the camel—had he
been compelled to bear on his back and shoulders the heavy burdens

of which they relieve him—man would have remained the miserable slave of his feeble organization. Borne down by the habitual disproportion between weight and strength, he would either have abandoned labour, have lived upon chance victims, without art or progress; or, rather, he would have lived as earth's everlasting Atlas—crooked, dragging, and drawing, with sunken head, never gazing on the sky, never thinking, never raising himself to the heights of invention.

Page 132. *On the power of insects.*—It is not only in the Tropical world that they are formidable; at the commencement of the last century half Holland perished because the piles which strengthen its dykes simultaneously gave way, invisibly undermined by a worm named the *taret.*

This redoubtable nibbler, which is often a foot in length, never betrays itself; it only works within. One morning the beam breaks, the framework yields, the ship engulfed founders in the waves.

How shall we reach, how discover it? A bird knows it—the lapwing, the guardian of Holland. And it is thus a notable imprudence to destroy, as has been done, his eggs. (Quatrefages, *Souvenirs d'un Naturaliste.*)

France, for more than a century, has suffered from the importation of a monster not less terrible—the *termite,* which devours dry wood just as the taret consumes wet wood. The single female of each swarm has the horrible fecundity of laying daily eighty thousand eggs. La Rochelle begins to fear the fate of that American city which is suspended in the air, the termites having devoured all its foundations, and excavated immense catacombs beneath.

In Guiana the dwellings of the termites are enormous hillocks, fifteen feet in height, which men venture to attack only from a distance, and by means of gunpowder. You may judge, therefore, the importance of the ant-eater, which dares to enter this gulf, and seek out the horrible female whence issues so accursed a torrent. (Smeathmann, *Mémoire sur les Termites.*)

Does climate save us? The termites prosper in France. Here, too, the cockchafer flourishes; and even on the northern slopes of the Alps, under the very breath of the glaciers, it devours vegetation. In the presence of such an enemy every insectivorous bird should be respected; at least, the canton of Vaud has recently placed the swallow under the protection of the law. (See the work of Tschudi.)

Page 134. *You frequently detect there a strong odour of musk.*— The plain of Cumana, says Humboldt, presents, after heavy rains, an extraordinary phenomenon. The earth, moistened and reheated by the sun's rays, gives forth that odour of musk which, under the torrid zone, is common to animals of very different classes—to the jaguar, the small species of the tiger-cat, the cabiai, the galinazo vulture, the crocodile, the viper, the rattlesnake. The gaseous emanations which are the vehicles of this aroma appear only to disengage themselves in proportion as the soil enclosing the *débris* of an innumerable quantity of reptiles, worms, and insects, becomes impregnated with water. Everywhere that one stirs up the soil, one is struck by the mass of organic substances which alternately develop, transform, or decompose. Nature in these climates appears more active, more prolific, one might say more lavish of life.

Pages 136, 137. *Humming-birds (or colibris).* — The eminent naturalists (Lesson, Azara, Stedmann, &c.) who have supplied so many excellent descriptions of these birds, are not, unfortunately, as rich in details of their manners, their food, their character.

As to the terrible unhealthiness of the places where they live (and live with so intense a life), the narratives of the old travellers— of Labat and others—are fully confirmed by the moderns. Messieurs Durville and Lesson, in their voyage to New Guiana, scarcely dared to cross the threshold of its profound virgin forests, with their strange and terrible beauty.

The most fantastic aspect of these forests—their prodigious fairy-like enchantment of nocturnal illumination by myriads of fire-flies— is attested and very forcibly described, as far as relates to the countries adjoining Panama, by a French traveller, M. Caqueray, who has recently visited them. (See his Journal in the new *Revue Française*, 10th June 1855.)

Page 153. *The valuable museum of anatomical collections*—that of Doctor Auzoux.—I cannot too warmly thank, on this occasion, our esteemed and skilful professor, who condescends to instruct us ignorant people, men of letters, men of the world, and women. He willed that anatomy should descend to all, should become popular; and it is done. His admirable imitations, his lucid demonstrations,

gradually work out that great revolution whose full extent can already be perceived. Shall I dare to tell men of science my inmost thought? They themselves will have an advantage in possessing always at hand these objects of study under so convenient a form and in enlarged proportions, which greatly diminish the fatigue of attention. A thousand objects, which seem to us different because different in size, recover their analogies, and reappear in their true relative forms, through the simple process of enlargement.

America, I may add, appears more keenly sensible of these advantages than we are. An American speculator had desired M. Auzoux to supply him yearly with two thousand copies of his figure of man, being certain of disposing of them in all the small towns, and even in the villages. Every American village, says M. Auzoux, endeavours to obtain a museum, an observatory, &c.

Page 157. *The suppression of pain.*—To prevent death is undoubtedly impossible; but we may prolong life. We may eventually render pain rarer, less cruel, and almost *suppress it.*

That the hardened old world laughs at our expression is so much the better. We saw quite such a spectacle in the days when our Europe, barbarized by war, centred all medical art in surgery, and made the knife her only means of cure, while young America discovered the miracle of that profound dream in which all pain is annihilated.*

* Our author refers to the discovery of the anæsthetic properties of ether by an American. It was a surgeon of old Europe, however, that gave the world the far more powerful anæsthetic of *chloroform.*-- *Translator.*

Page 157. *The useful equilibrium of life and death.*—Numerous species of birds no longer make a halt in France. One with difficulty descries them flying at inaccessible elevations, deploying their wings in haste, accelerating their passage, saying, — " Pass on, pass on quickly ! Let us avoid the land of death, the land of destruction !"

Provence, and many other departments in the south, are barren deserts, peopled by every living tribe, and therefore vegetable nature is sadly impoverished. You do not interrupt with impunity the natural harmonies. The bird levies a tax on the plant, but he is its protector.

It is a matter of notoriety that the bustard has almost disappeared from Champagne and Provence. The heron has passed away ; the stork is rare. As we gradually encroach upon the soil, these species, partial to dusty wastes and morasses, depart to seek a livelihood elsewhere. Our progress in one sense is our poverty. In England the same fact has been observed. (See the excellent articles on Sport and Natural History, translated from Messrs. St. John, Knox, Gosse, and others, in the *Revue Britannique.*) The heath-cock retires before the step of the cultivator ; the quail passes into Ireland. The ranks of the herons grow daily thinner before the *utilitarian improvements* of the nineteenth century. But to these causes we must add the barbarism of man, which so heedlessly destroys a throng of innocent species. Nowhere, says M. Pavie, a French traveller, is game more timid than in our fields.

Woe to the ungrateful people ! And by this phrase I mean the sporting crowd who, unmindful of the numerous benefits we owe to animals, have exterminated innocent life. A terrible sentence of the Creator weighs upon the tribes of sportsmen,—*they can create nothing.*

They originate no art, no industry. They have added nothing to the hereditary patrimony of the human species. What has their heroism profited the Indians of North America? Having organized nothing, having accomplished nothing permanent, these races, despite their singular energy, have disappeared from the earth before inferior men, the last emigrants of Europe.

Do not believe the axiom that huntsmen gradually develop into agriculturists. It is not so—they kill or die; such is their whole destiny. We see it clearly through experience. He who has killed, will kill; he who has created, will create.

In the want of emotion which every man suffers from his birth, the child who satisfies it habitually by murder, by a miniature ferocious drama of surprise and treason, of the torture of the weak, will find no great enjoyment in the gentle and tranquil emotions arising from the progressive success of toil and study, from the limited industry which does everything itself. To create, to destroy—these are the two raptures of infancy : to create is a long, slow process ; to destroy is quick and easy. The least act of creation implies those best gifts of the Creator and of kindly Nature : gentleness and patience.

It is a shocking and hideous thing to see a child partial to "sport;" to see woman enjoying and admiring murder, and encouraging her child. That delicate and sensitive woman would not give him a knife, but she gives him a gun : kill at a distance—be it so ! for we do not see the suffering. And this mother will think it admirable that her son, kept confined to his room, shall drive off *ennui* by plucking the wings from flies, by torturing a bird or a little dog.

Far-seeing mother! She will know when too late the evil of having formed a hard heart. Aged and weak, rejected of the world, she will experience in her turn her son's brutality.

*   *   *   *   *   *

But rifle practice? They will object to you. Must not the child grow skilful in killing, that, from murder to murder, he may at last arrive at the surpassing feat of killing the flying swallow? The only country in Europe where everybody knows how to handle a musket is that where the bird is least exposed to slaughter. The land of William Tell knew how to place before her children a juster and more exalted object when they liberated their country.

*   *   *   *   *   *

France is not cruel. Why, then, this love of murder, this extermination of the animal world ?

It is the *impatient people*, the *young people*, the *childish people*, in a rude and restless childhood. If they cannot be doing in creating, they will be doing by destroying.

But what they most fatally injure is—themselves ! A violent education, stormily impassioned in love or severity, crushes in the child, withers, chokes up the first moral flower of natural sensitiveness, all that was purest of the maternal milk, the germ of universal love which rarely blooms again.

Among too many children we are saddened by their almost incredible sterility. A few recover from it in the long circle of life, when they have become experienced and enlightened men. But the first freshness of the heart ? It shall return no more.*

How is it that this nation, otherwise born under such felicitous circumstances, is, with rare and local exceptions, accursed with so singular an incapacity for harmony ? It has its own peculiar songs, its charming little melodies of vivacity and mirth. But it needs a prolonged effort, a special education, to attain to harmony.

Page 158. *Flattening of the brain.*—The weight of the brain, compared with that of the body, is, in the

Ostrich, in the ratio of	1 to 1200
Goose,	1 to 360
Duck,	1 to 257
Eagle,	1 to 160

* Compare Byron, in " Don Juan."

Plover, ... 1 to 122
Falcon, ... 1 to 102
Paroquet. .... 1 to 45
Robin, ... 1 to 32
Jay, ... 1 to 28
Chaffinch, cock, sparrow, goldfinch, ... 1 to 25
Hooded tomtit, ... 1 to 16
Blue-cap tomtit, ... 1 to 12

(Estimate of Haller and Leuret.)

Page 158. *The noble falcon.* — The *noble* birds (the falcon, ger-falcon, saker) are those which *hold* their prey by the *talon*, and kill it with the bill : their bill, for this purpose, is toothed. The *ignoble* birds (the eagle, the kite, &c.) are for the most part swift of flight (*voiliers*) : these employ their talons to rend and choke their victims. The *rameurs* rise with difficulty, which enables the *voiliers* to escape them the more easily. The tactics of the former are to feign, in the first place, to rise to a great height ; and then, by suffering themselves to drop, they disconcert the manœuvres of the *voiliers.* (Huber, *Vol des Oiseaux de Proie*, 1784, 4to. He was the first of that clever lineage, Huber of the birds, Huber of the bees, Huber of the ants.)

Page 177. *Its happiness in the morning, when terrors vanish !* — "Before" (says Tschudi) "the vermeil tints of the early dew have announced the approach of the sun, oftentimes before even the lightest gleam has heralded dawn in the east, while the stars still sparkle in

the sombre azure of heaven, a low murmur resounds on the summit of a venerable pine, and is speedily followed by a more or less distinct prattling; then the notes arise, and an interminable series of keen sounds strike the air on every side like a clang of swords continually hurtled one against another. It is the coupling time of the wood-cock. With his eye a-flame, he dances and springs on the branch, while below him, in the copse, his hens repose tranquilly, and rever-ently contemplate the mad antics of their lord and master. He is not long left alone to animate the forest. The mavis rises in his turn, shaking the dew from his glittering feathers. Behold him whetting his bill upon the branch, and leaping from bough to bough, up to the very crest of the maple tree where he has slept, astonished to find nearly all life still slumbering in the forest, though the dawn has taken the place of night. Twice, thrice, he hurls his *fanfare* at the echoes of the mountain and the valley, which a dense mist still envelopes.

"Thin columns of white smoke escape from the roof of the cot-tages; the dogs bark around the farm-yards; and the bells ring, suspended to the neck of the cow. The birds now quit their thickets, flutter their wings, and dart into the air to salute the sun, which once more comes to bless them with his bounteous light. More than one poor little sparrow rejoices that he has escaped the perils of the darkness. Perched on a little twig, he had trusted to enjoy his slumber without alarm, his head buried beneath his wing, when, by the ray of a star, he discerned the noiseless screech-owl gliding through the trees, intent upon some misdeed. The pole-cat stole from the valley-depth, the ermine descended from the rock, the pine-marten quitted his nest, the fox prowled among the bushes. All these enemies the poor little one watched during this terrible night. On his tree, on the earth, in the air—destruction menaced him on every side. How long, how long were the hours when, not daring to move, his only protection was the young leaves which screened him! And now, how great the pleasure to ply his unfettered wing, to live in safety, protected, defended by the light!

"The chaffinch raises with all his energy his clear and sonorous note; the robin sings from the summit of the larch, the goldfinch amid the alder-groves, the blackbird and the bullfinch beneath the leafy arbours. The tomtit, the wren, and the troglodyte mingle their voices. The stockdove coos, and the woodpecker smites his tree. But far above these joyous utterances re-echo the melodious strains of the woodlark and the inimitable song of the thrush."

Page 185. *Migrations.*—For the famished Arab, the lank inhabitant of the desert, the arrival of the migrating birds, weary and heavy at this season, and, therefore, easy to catch, is a blessing from God, a celestial manna. The Bible tells us of the raptures of the Israelites, when, during their wanderings in Arabia Petræa, fasting and enfeebled, they suddenly saw descending upon them the winged food: not the locusts of abstemious Elias, not the bread with which the raven nourished his bowels, but the quail heavy with fat, delicious and yet substantial, which voluntarily fell into their hands. They ate to repletion; and no longer regretted the rich flesh-pots of Pharaoh.

I willingly excuse the gluttony of the famished. But what shall I say of our people, in the richest countries of Europe, who, after harvest and vintage-time, with barns and cellars brimming full, pursue with no less fury these poor travellers? Since thin or fat, they are equally good, our epicures would eat even the swallows; they devour the song-birds, "those which have only a voice." Their wild frenzy dooms the nightingale to the spit, plucks and kills the household guest, the poor robin, which yesterday fed from their hands.

The migration season is a season of slaughter. The law which impels southwards the tribes of birds is, for millions, a law of death.

Many depart, few return; at each stage of their route they must pay a tribute of blood. The eagle waits on his crag, man watches in the valley. He who escapes the tyrant of the air, falls a victim to the tyrant of the earth. "A fortunate opportunity!" exclaims the child or the sportsman, the ferocious child with whom murder is a jest. "God has willed it so!" mutters the pious glutton; "let us be resigned!" These are the judgments of man upon the carnival of massacre. As yet we know nothing more, for history has not written the opinions of the massacred.

Migrations are exchanges for every country (except the poles, at the epoch of winter). The particular condition of climate or food, which decides the departure of one species of birds, is precisely that which determines the arrival of another species. When the swallow quits us at the autumn rains, we note the arrival of the army of plovers and peewits in quest of the lobworms driven from their lurking-places by the floods. In October, and as the cold increases, the green-finches, the yellow-hammers, the wrens, replace the song-birds which have deserted us. The snipes and partridges descend from their moun-tains at the moment when the quail and the thrush emigrate towards the south. It is then, too, that the legions of the aquatic species quit the extreme north for those temperate climes where the seas, the lakes, and the pools, do not freeze. The wild geese, the swans, the divers, the ducks, the teal, cleave the air in battle array, and swoop down upon the lakes of Scotland and Hungary, and our marshes of the south. The delicate stork flies southward, when his cousin, the

crane, sets out from the north, where his supplies begin to fail him. Passing over our lands, he pays us tribute by delivering us from the last reptiles and batrachians which a warm autumnal breeze has restored to life.

Page 188. *My muse is the light.*—And yet the nightingale loses it when he returns to us from Asia. But all true artists require that it should be softly ordered, blended with rays and shadows. Rembrandt in his paintings has exhausted the effects, at once warm and soft, of the science of chiaro-oscuro. The nightingale begins his song when the gloom of evening mingles with the last beams of the sun; and hence it is that we tremble at his voice. Our soul in the misty and uncertain hours of the gloaming regains possession of the inner light.

Page 215. *Do not say, " Winter is on my side."*—While M. de Custine was travelling in Russia, he tells us that, at the fair of Nijni-Novgorod, he was frightened by the multitude of *blattes* which thronged his chamber, with an infectious smell, and which could not be got rid of. Dr. Tschudi, a careful traveller, who has explored Switzerland in its smallest details, assures us that at the breath of the south wind, which melts the snow in twelve hours, innumerable hosts of cockchafers ravage the country. They are not a less terrible scourge than the locusts to the south.

During our Italian tour, my wife and I made an observation which will not have escaped the notice of naturalists; namely, that the cockchafer does not die in autumn. From the inhabited portions of our palazzo, almost entirely shut up in winter, we saw clouds of these insects emerge in the spring, which had slept peacefully in expectation of its warmth. Moreover, in that country, even ephemeral insects do not perish. Gigantic gnats waged war against us every night, demanding our blood with sharp and strident voice.

If, by the side of these proofs of the multiplication of insects, even in temperate or cold countries, we put the fact that the swallow is not satisfied with less than one thousand flies *per diem;* that a couple of sparrows carry home to their young four thousand three hundred caterpillars or beetles weekly; a tomtit three hundred daily; we see at once the evil and the remedy. We quote these figures from M. Quatrefages (*Souvenirs*), and from a letter written by Mr. Walter Trevelyan to the editor of "The Birds of Great Britain," translated in the *Revue Britannique,* July 7, 1850.

I offer the reader a very incomplete summary of the services rendered to us by the birds of our climate.

Many are the assiduous guardians of our herds. The heron *garde-bœuf,* making use of his bill as a lancet, cuts the flesh of the ox to extract from it a parasitical worm which sucks the blood and life of the animal. The wagtails and the starlings render very similar services to our cattle. The swallows destroy myriads of winged insects which never rest, and which we see dancing in the sun's rays ; gnats, midges, flies. The goat-suckers and the martinets, twilight hunters, effect the disappearance of the cockchafers, the gnats, the moths, and a swarm of nibbling insects (*rongeurs*), which work only by night. The magpie hunts after the insects which, concealed beneath the bark of the tree, live upon its sap. The humming-bird, the fly-catcher, the *soui-mangas,* in tropical countries, purify the chalice of the flower. The bee-eater, in all lands, carries on a fierce hostility against the wasps which ruin our fruit. The goldfinch, partial to uncultivated soil and the seeds of the thistle, prevents the latter from spreading over the ground. Our garden birds, the chaffinches, blackcaps, blackbirds, tits, strip our fruit-bushes and great trees of the grubs, caterpillars, and beetles, whose ravages would be incalculable. A large number of these insects remain during winter in the egg or the larva, waiting for spring to burst into life ; but in this state they are diligently hunted up by the mavis, the wren, the troglodyte. The former turn over the leaves which strew the earth ; the latter climb to the loftiest branches, or clear out the trunk. In wet meadows, you may see the crows and storks boring the ground to seize on the white worm (*ver blanc*) which, for three years before metamorphosing into a cockchafer, gnaws at the roots of our grasses.

Here we pause, not to weary our reader, and yet the list of useful birds is scarcely glanced at.

Page 228. *The woodpecker, as an augur.*—Are the methods of observation adopted by meteorology serious and efficacious? Some men of science doubt it. It might, perhaps, be worth while examining if we could not deduce any part of the meteorology of the ancients from their divination by birds. The principal passages are pointed out in Pauly's Encyclopædia (Stuttgard), article *Divinatio*.

"The woodpecker is a favoured bird in the steppes of Poland and Russia. In these sparsely wooded plains he constantly directs his course towards the trees.; by following him, you discover a hidden ravine, a little later some springs, and finally descend towards the river. Under the bird's guidance you may thus explore and reconnoitre the country." (Mickiewicz, *Les Slaves*, vol. i., p. 200.)

Page 235. *Song.*—Do not separate those whom God has joined together. If you place a bird in a cage beside you, his song quickly fatigues you with its sonorous timbre and its monotony. But in the grand concert of Nature, that bird would supply his note, and complete the harmony. This powerful voice would subdue itself to the modulations of the air ; soft and tender it would glide, borne upon the breeze.

And then, in the deep woody depths, the singer incessantly moves from place to place, now drawing near, and now receding; hence arise those distant effects which induce a delightful reverie, and that delicate cadence which thrills the heart.

Under our roof his song would be ever the same; but on the pinions of the wind the music is divine, it penetrates and ravishes the soul.

Page 241. *The robin hastens, singing, to enjoy his share of the warmth.*—I find this admirable passage in "The Conquest of England by the Normans" (by Augustin Thierry). The chief of the barbarous Saxons assembles his priests and wise men to ascertain if they will become Christians. One of them speaks as follows:—

"Thou mayst remember, O king, a thing which sometimes happens, when thou art seated at table with thy captains and men-at-arms, in the winter season, and when a fire is kindled and the hall well warmed, while there are wind and rain and snow without. There comes a little bird, which traverses the room on fluttering wing, entering by one door and flying out at another: the moment of its

passage is full of sweetness for it, it feels neither the rain nor the storm; but this interval is brief, the bird vanishes in the twinkling of an eye, and *from winter passes away into winter.* Such seems to me the life of man upon this earth, and its limited duration, compared with the length of the time which precedes and follows it."

From winter he passes into winter. "Of wintra in winter eft cymeth."

Page 247. *Nests and Hatching.*—In the vast extent of the islands linking India to Australia, a species of bird of the family *Gallinaceœ* dispenses with the labour of hatching her eggs. Raising an enormous hillock of grasses whose fermentation will produce a degree of heat favourable to the process, the parents, as soon as this task is completed, trust to Nature for the reproduction of their kind. Mr. Gould, who furnishes these curious details, speaks also of some curious nests constructed by another species of bird. It consists of an avenue formed by small branches planted in the ground, and woven together at their upper extremities in the fashion of a dome. The structure is consolidated by enlaced and intertwined herbs. This first stage of their labour accomplished, the artists proceed to the work of decoration. They seek in every direction, and often at a distance, the gaudiest feathers, the finest polished shells, and the most brilliant stones, to strew over the entrance. This avenue would seem, however, not to be the nest, but the place where the birds hold their first rendezvous. (See the coloured plates in Mr. Gould's magnificent volume, "Australian Birds.")

Page 266. *Instinct and Reason.*—The ignorant and inattentive think all things *nearly alike.* And Science perceives that all things differ. According as we learn to observe, do these differences become apparent; that imperceptible "shade," and worthless "almost," which at the outset does not prevent us from confusing all things with one another, really distinguishes them, and points out a notable discrepancy, a wide interval betwixt this object and that, a blank, a *hiatus*, sometimes an enormous abyss, which separates and holds them apart.

—so much so, that occasionally between these things, at first sight *so nearly alike*, a whole world will intervene, without the power of bringing them together.

It has been asserted and repeated that the works of insects presented an absolute similarity, a mechanical regularity. And yet our Reaumurs and our Hubers have discovered numerous facts which positively contradict this pretended symmetry, especially in the case of the ant, whose life is complicated with so many incidents, so many unforeseen exigencies, that she would never provide against them but for the rapid discernment, the promptitude of mind, which is one of the most striking characteristics of her individuality.

It has been supposed that the nests of birds are always constructed on identical principles. Not at all. A close observation reveals the fact that they differ according to the climate and the weather. At New York, the baltimore makes a closely fitted nest, to shelter him from the cold. At New Orleans his nest is left with a free passage for the air to diminish the heat. The Canadian partridges, which in winter cover themselves with a kind of small pent-roof at Compiègne, under a milder sky do away with this protection, because they judge it to be useless. The same discernment prevails in relation to the seasons. The American spring, in the opening years of the present century, occurring very late, the woodpecker (of Wilson) wisely made his nest two weeks later. I will venture to add that I have seen, in southern France, this delicate appreciation of climatic changes varying from year to year; by an inexplicable foresight, when the summer was likely to be cold, the nests were always more thickly woven.

The guillemot of the north (*mergula*), which fears above all things the fox, on account of his partiality for her eggs, builds her nest on a rock level with the water, so that, no sooner are they hatched than the brood, however closely dogged by the plunderer, have time to escape in the waves. On the other hand, here, on our coasts, where her only enemy is man, she makes her nest on the loftiest and most precipitous cliffs, where man can with difficulty reach it.

Ignorant persons, and no less those naturalists who study natural
history in books only, acknowledge the differences existing between
species, but believe that the actions and labours of the individuals of
a species invariably correspond.   Such a view is possible when you
have seen things only from above and afar, in a sublime generality.
But when the naturalist takes in hand his pilgrim's staff—when, as
a modest, resolute, indefatigable pilgrim of Nature, he assumes his
shoes of iron—all things change their aspect : he sees, notes, com-
pares numerous individual works in the labours of each species, seizes
their points of difference, and soon arrives at the conclusion which
logic had already suggested,—that, in truth, *no one thing resembles
another*.   In those works which appear identical to inexperienced
eyes, a Wilson and an Audubon have detected the diversities of an art
very variable—according to means and places, according to the
characters and talents of the artists—in a spontaneous infinity.   So
extensive is the region of liberty, fancy, and *ingegno*.

Let us hope that our collections will bring together several
specimens of each species, arranged and classified according to the
talent and progress of the individual, recording as near as may be the
age of the birds which constructed the nests.

If these boundless diversities do not result from unrestrained activity and personal spontaneity, if you wish to refer them all to an identical instinct, you must, to support so miraculous a theory, make us
believe another miracle : that this instinct, although identical, possesses the singular elasticity of accommodating and proportioning
itself to a variety of circumstances which are incessantly changing, to
an infinity of hazardous chances.

What, then, will be the case if we find, in the history of animals,
such an act of pretended instinct as supposes a resistance to that very
course our instinctive nature would apparently desire ?   What will
you say to the wounded elephant spoken of by Fouché d'Obsonville ?

That judicious traveller, so utterly disinclined to romantic ten-
dencies, saw an elephant in India, which, having been wounded in
battle, went daily to the hospital that his wound might be dressed.

Now, guess what this wound might be. A burn. In this dangerous Indian climate, where everything grows putrid, they are frequently constrained to cauterize the sores. He endured this treatment patiently, and went every day to undergo it. He felt no antipathy towards the surgeon who inflicted upon him so sharp an agony. He groaned; nothing more. He evidently understood that it was done for his benefit; that his torturer was his friend; that this necessary cruelty was designed for his cure.

Plainly this elephant acted upon reflection, and upon a blind instinct; he acted against nature in the strength and enlightenment of his will.

Page 270. *The master-nightingale.*—I owe this anecdote to a lady well entitled to a judgment upon such questions—to Madame Garcia Viardot (the great singer). The Russian peasants, who possess a fine ear and a keen sensibility for Nature (compared with her harshness towards them), said, when they occasionally heard the Spanish *cantatrice:* "The nightingale does not sing so well."

Page 273. *Still the little one hesitates, &c.*—"One day I was walking with my son in the neighbourhood of Montier. We perceived towards the north, on the Little Salève, an eagle emerging from the

windings of the rocks.   When he was tolerably near the Great Salève
he halted, and two eaglets, which he had carried on his back, attempted to fly, at first very close to their teacher, and in narrow
circles ; then, a few minutes afterwards, feeling fatigued, they
returned to rest upon his back.   Gradually their essays were protracted, and at the close of the lesson the eaglets effected some much
more important flights, still under the eyes of their teacher of gym-
nastics.   After about an hour's occupation the two scholars resumed
their post on the paternal back, and the eagle returned to the rock
from which he had started."   (M. Chenvières, of Geneva.)

Page 304. *The small Chili falcon* (cernicula).—I extract this
statement from a new, curious, but little known work, written in
French by a Chilian : *Le Chili*, by B. Vicuna Mackenna (ed. 1855,
p. 100).   Chili I take to be a most interesting country, which, by
the energy of its citizens, should considerably modify the unfavour-
able opinion entertained by the citizens of the United States in
reference to South Americans.   America will not exist as a world, so
long as a common feeling shall be wanting between the two opposite
poles which ought to create her majestic harmony.

Final Note on the Winged Life.—To appreciate beings so alien from the conditions of our prosaic existence, we must for a moment abandon earth, and become a sense apart. We get a glimpse of something inferior and superior, of something on this side and on that, the limbs of the animal life on the borders of the life of the angels. In proportion as we assume this sense, we lose the temptation of degrading the winged life—that strange, delicate, mighty dream of God—to the vulgarities of earth.

To-day even, in a place infinitely unpoetic, neglected, squalid, and obscure, among the black mud of Paris, and in the dank darkness of an apartment scarcely better than a cavern, I saw, and I heard chirping, in a subdued voice, a little creature which seemed not to belong to this low world.   It was a warbler, and one of a common species—not the blackcap, which is prized so highly for his song.   This one was not then singing ; she chattered to herself, just a few notes, as monotonous as her situation.   For winter, shadow, captivity, all were around her.   The captive of a rough, rude man, of a speculator in birds, she heard on every side sounds which silenced her song ; powerful voices were above her head, a mocking-bird among them, which rang out every moment their brilliant clarions.   Generally, she would be condemned to silence.   She was accustomed, one could perceive, to sing in a low tone.   But in this limited flight, this habitual resignation and half lamentation, might be detected a charming delicacy, a more than feminine softness (*morbidezza*).   Add to this the unique grace of her bosom and her motions, of her modest red and white attire, which sparkled, however, with a bright sheeny reflex.

I recalled to my mind the pictures in which Ingres and Delacroix have shown us the captives of Algiers or the East, and exactly depicted the dull resignation, the indifference, the weariness of their monotonous lives, and also the decline (must we say the extinction ?) of the inner fire.

But, alas! it was wholly different here.   The flame burned in all its strength.   She was more and less than a woman.   No comparison was of any use.   Inferior by right of her animal nature, by her

pretty bird-masquerade, she was lifted above by her wings, and by
the winged soul which sang in that little body.   An all-powerful *alibi*
held her enthralled afar off, in her native grove, in the cradle whence
she had been stolen in her infancy, or in the love-nest that she
dreamed of as hers.   She warbled a few notes, which so kindled my
very soul, that I myself, for the moment, seemed furnished with
wings, and accompanied her in her distant dream.

Analysis of Subjects.

---o---

INTRODUCTION.

PART FIRST.

PART SECOND.

CONCLUSION.

ILLUSTRATIVE NOTES.

Index.

―――――o―――――